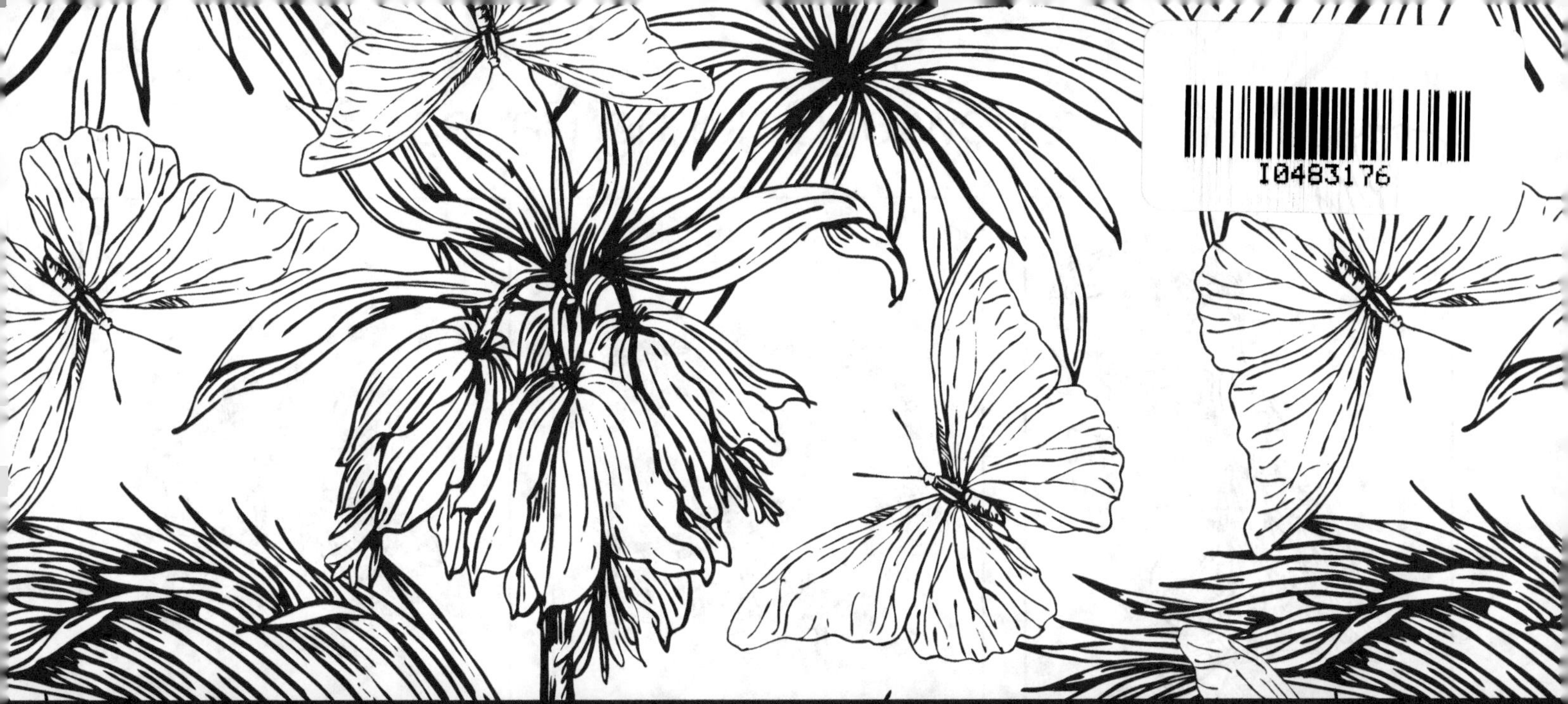

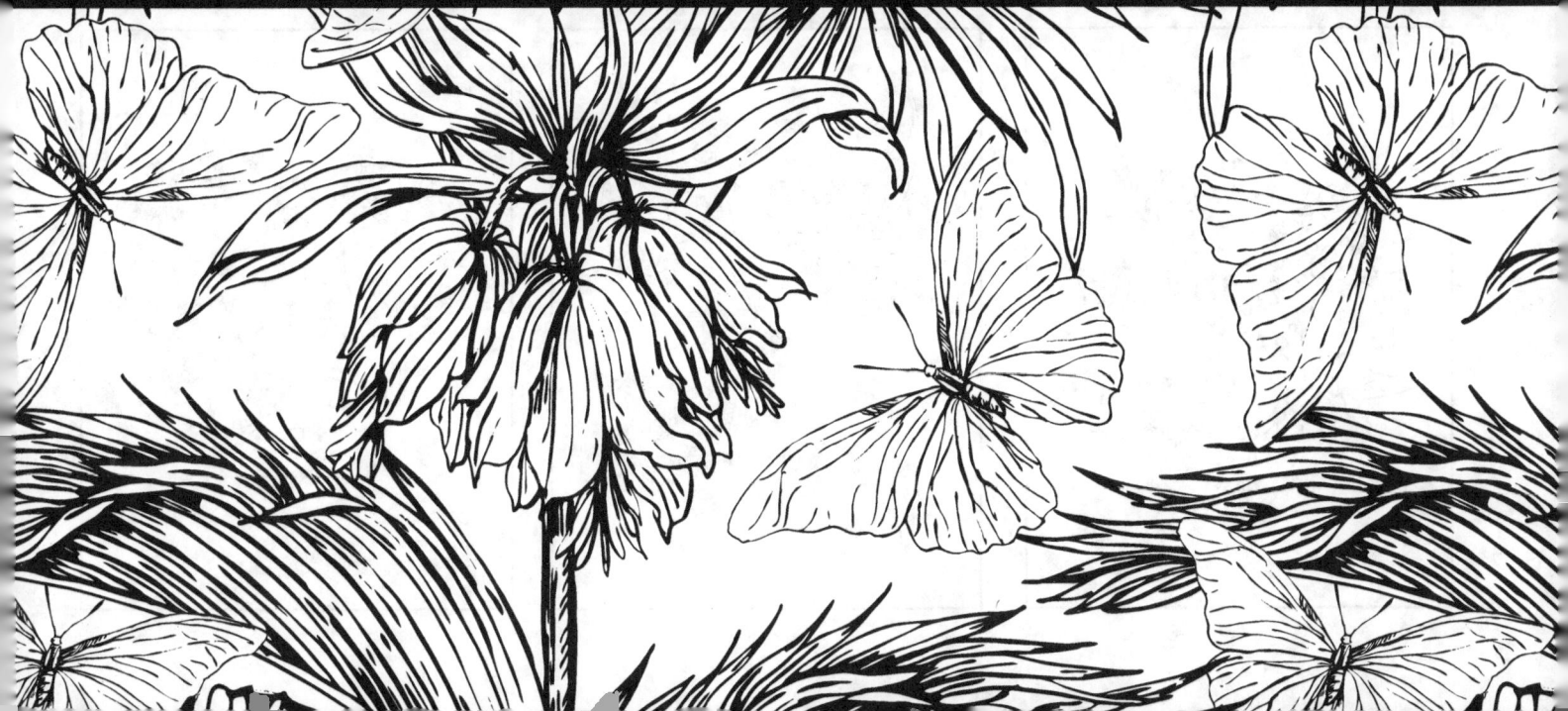

COLORING BOOKS
FOR RELAXATION
ANTI-STRESS DESIGNS

ART THERAPY COLORING

Preview of Coloring Pages

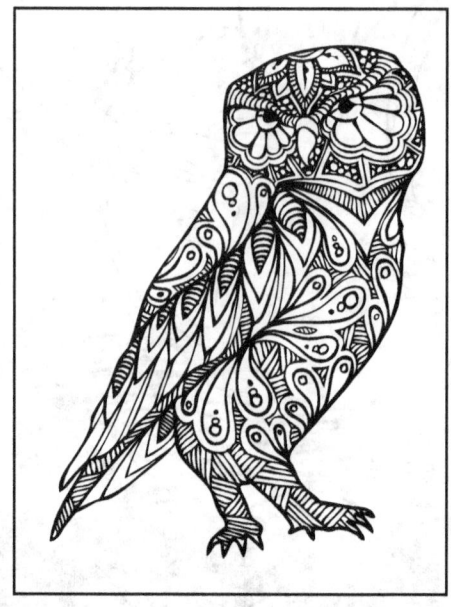
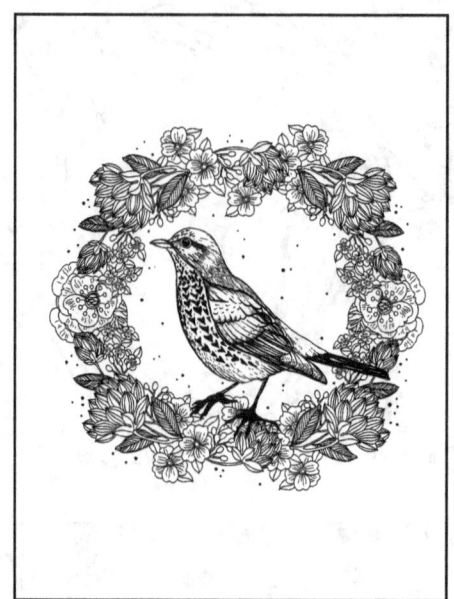
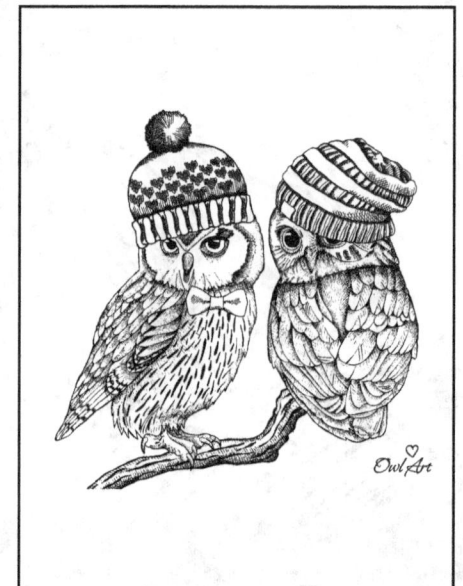
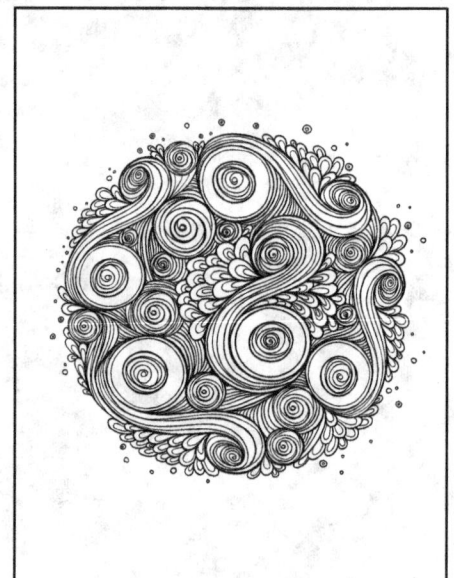
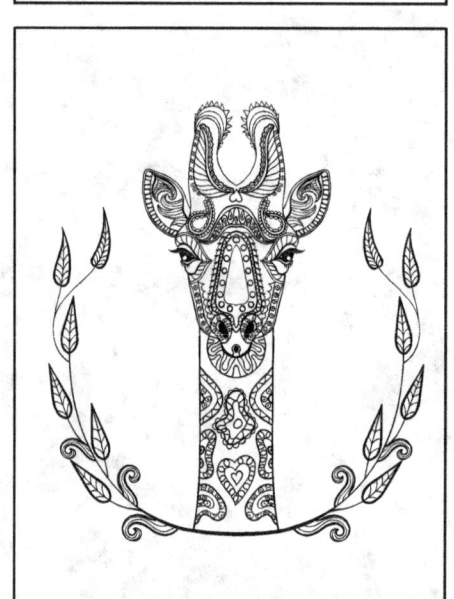
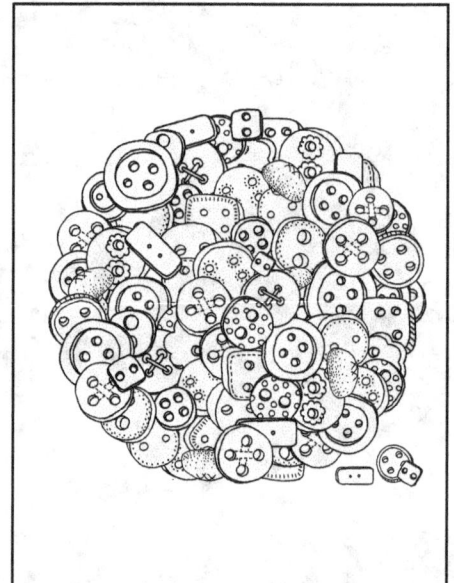
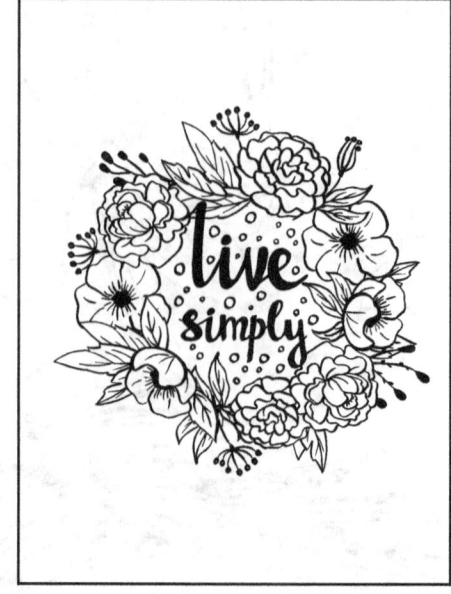
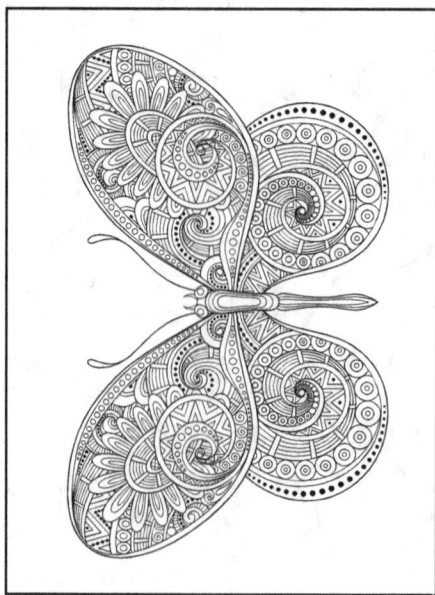
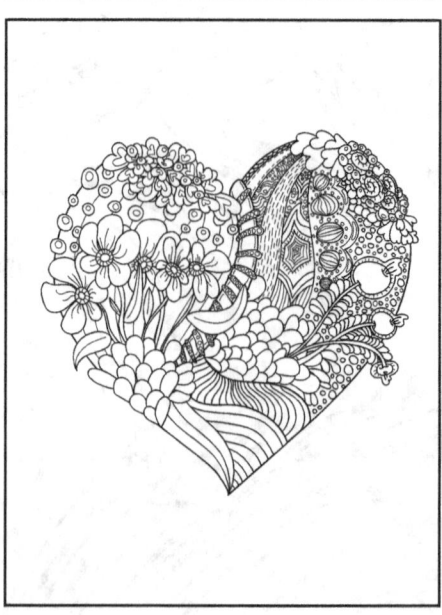

www.arttherapycoloring.com

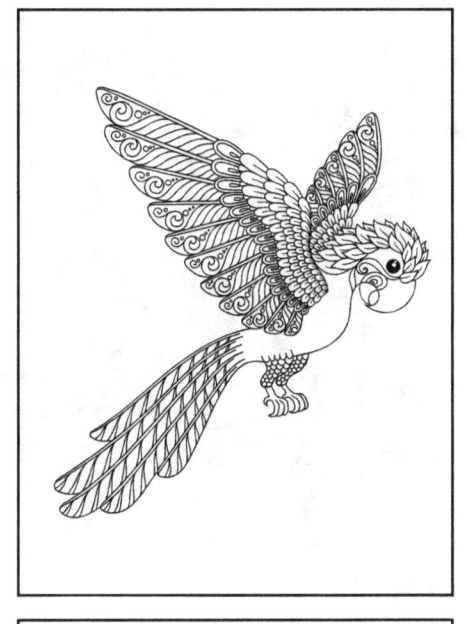
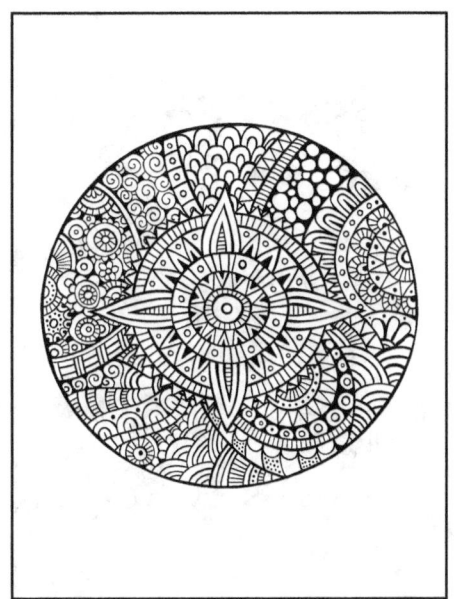
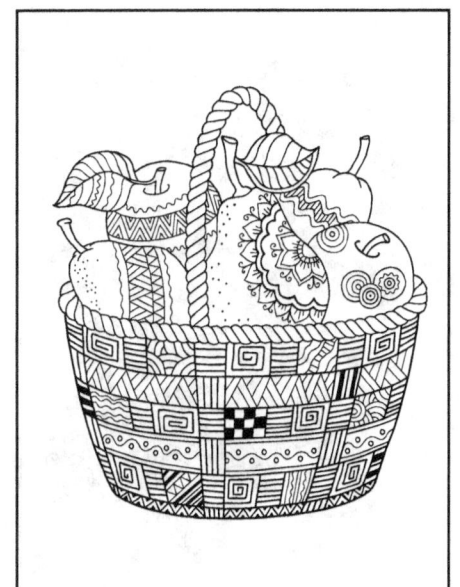
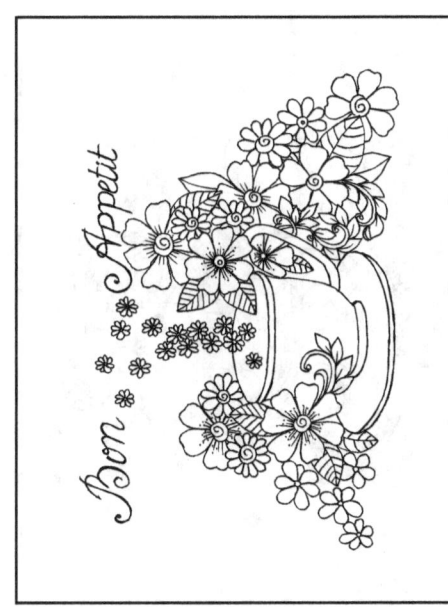
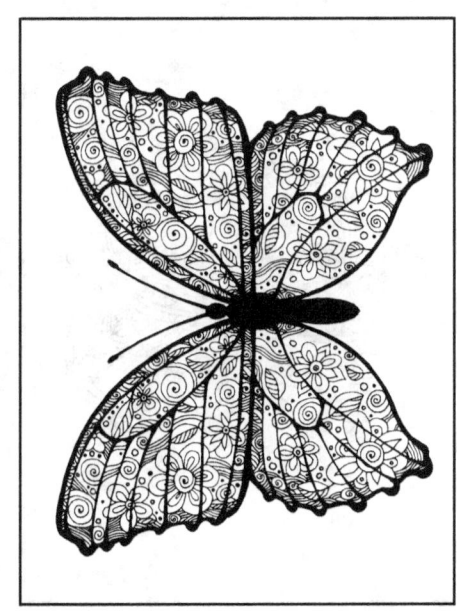
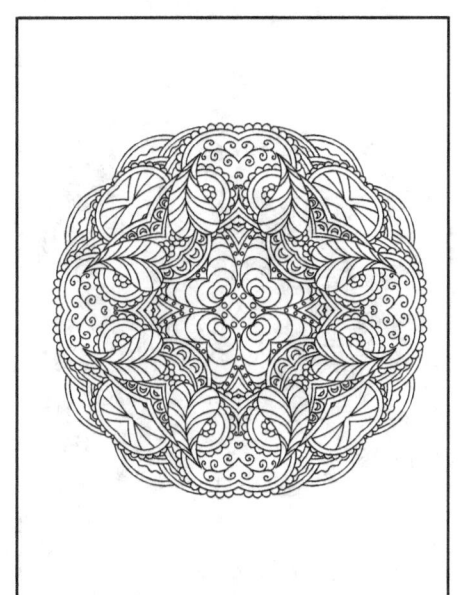
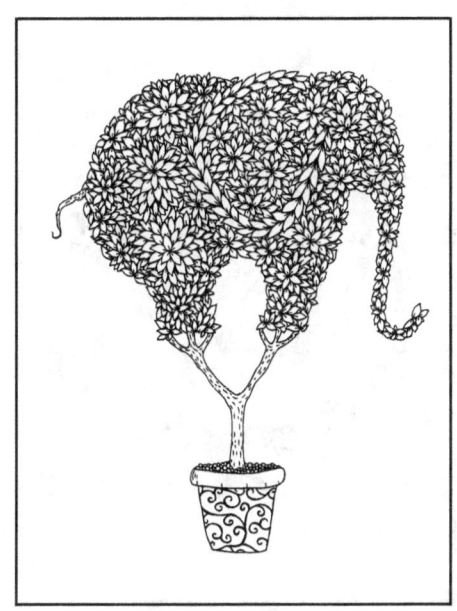
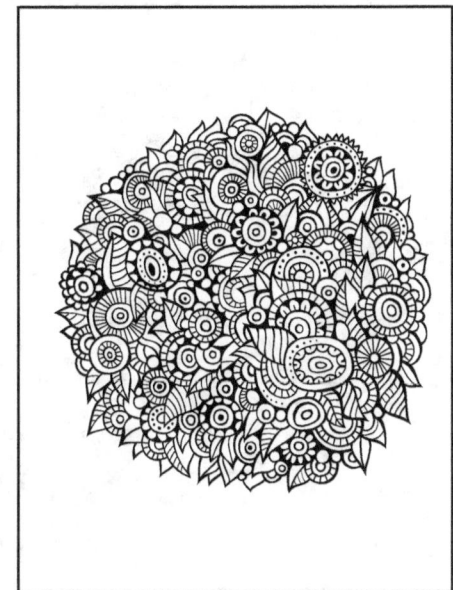
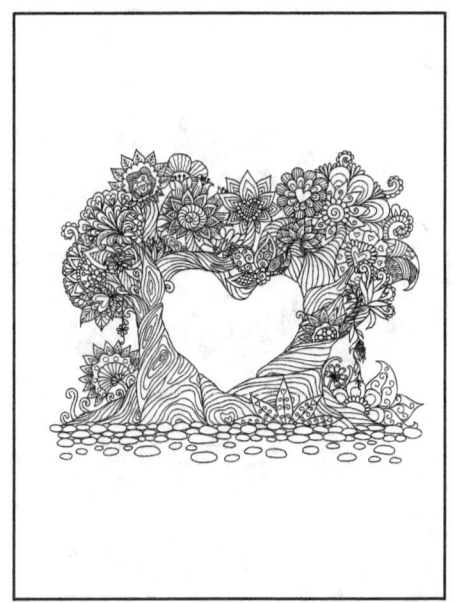

Preview of Coloring Pages

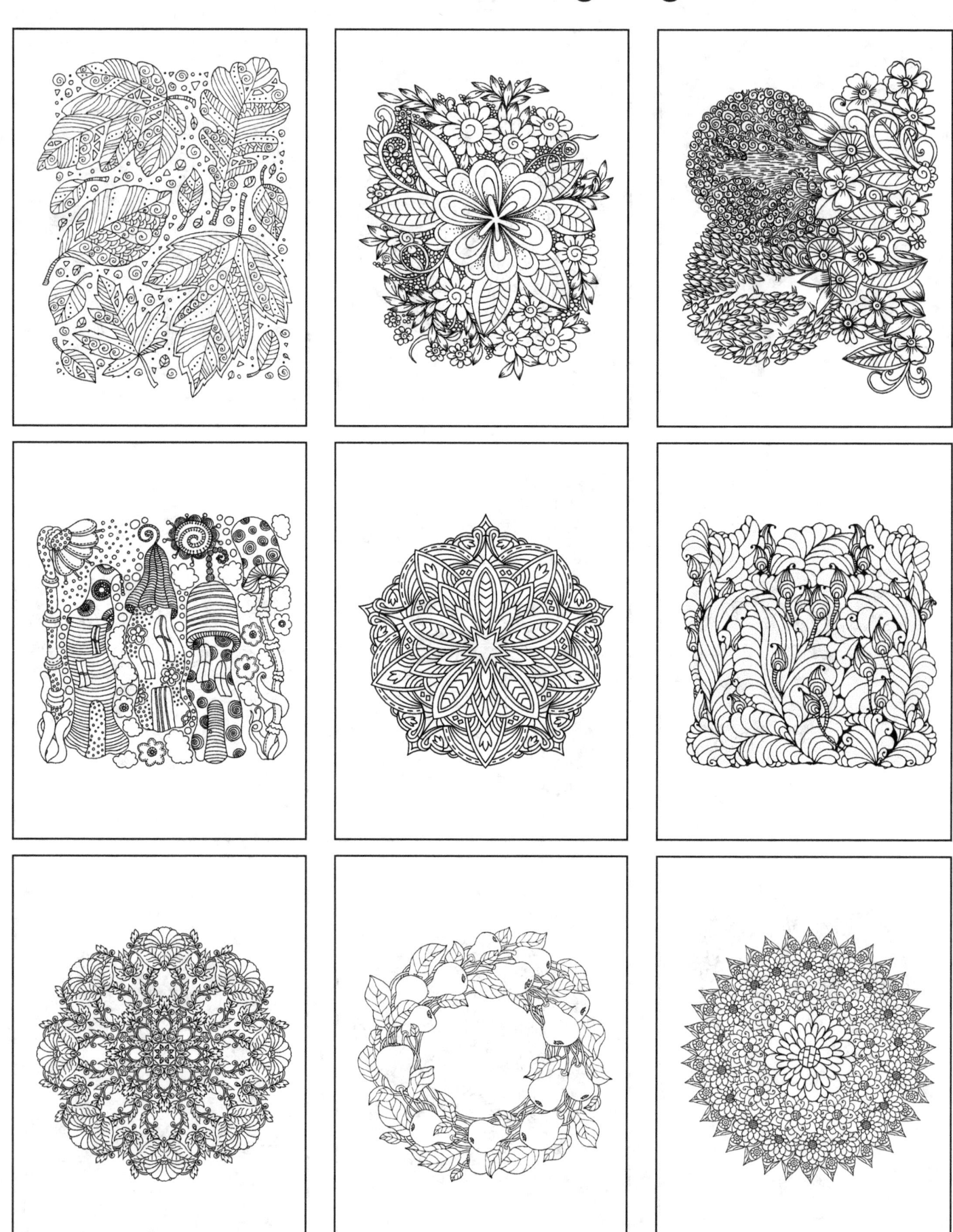

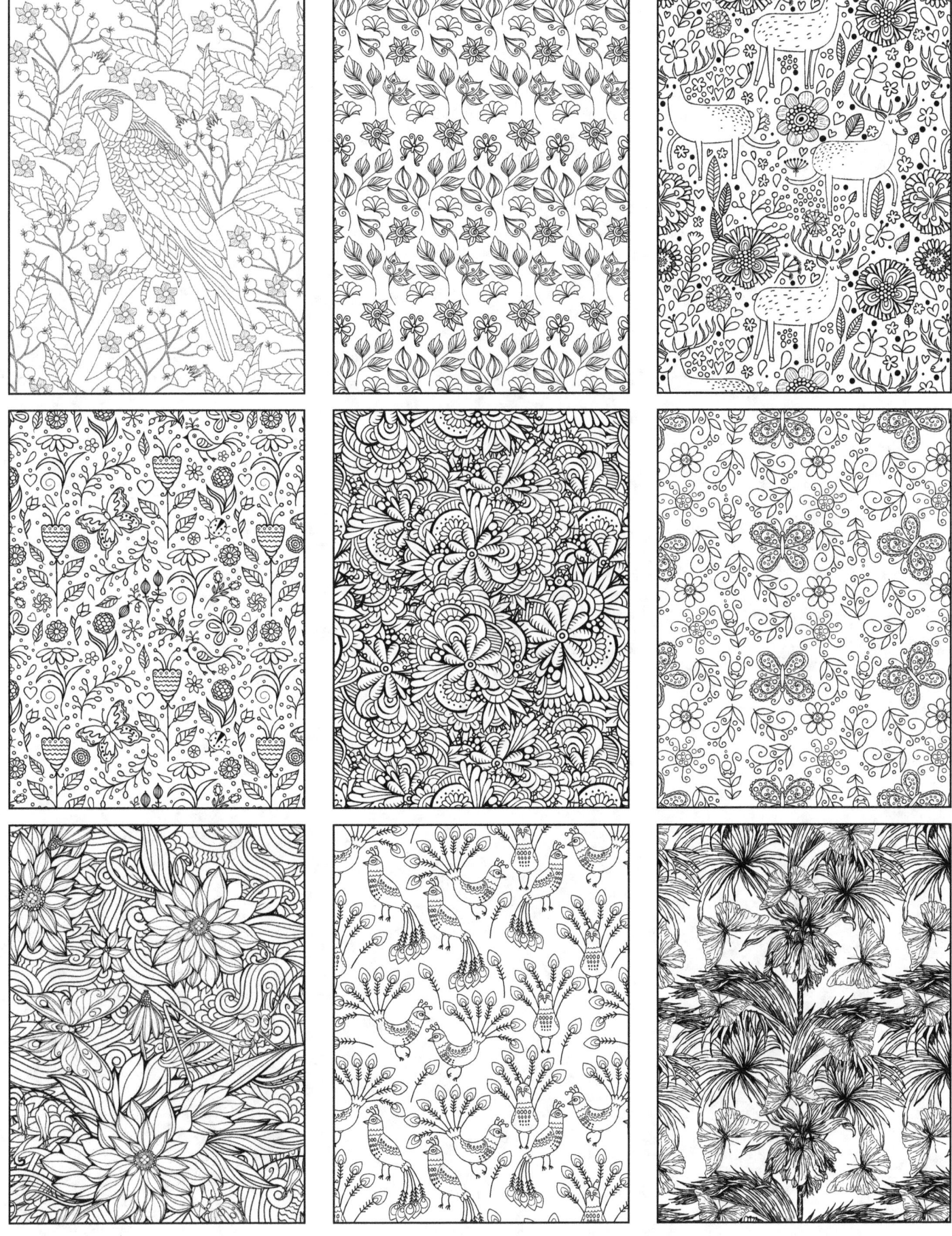

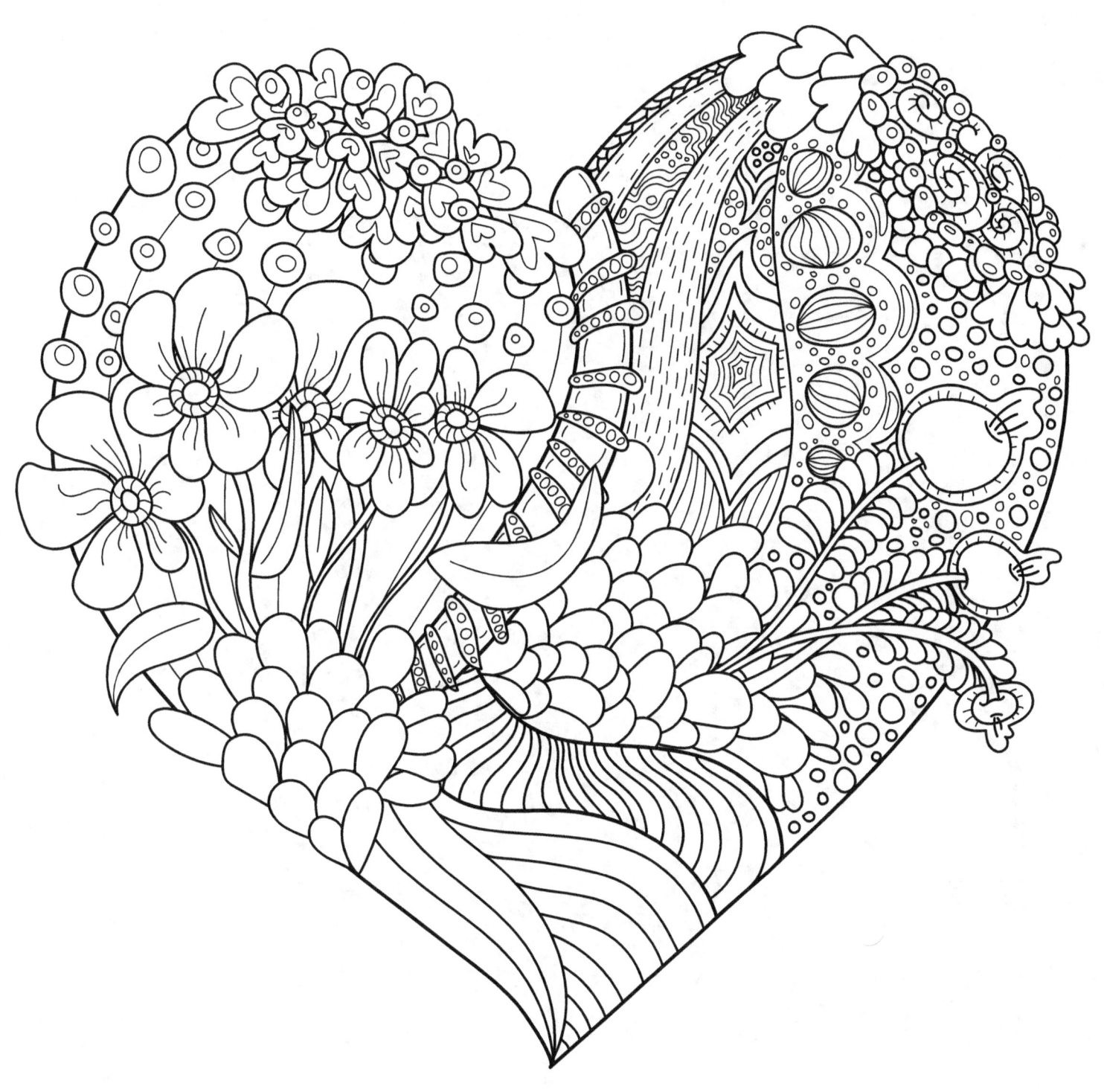

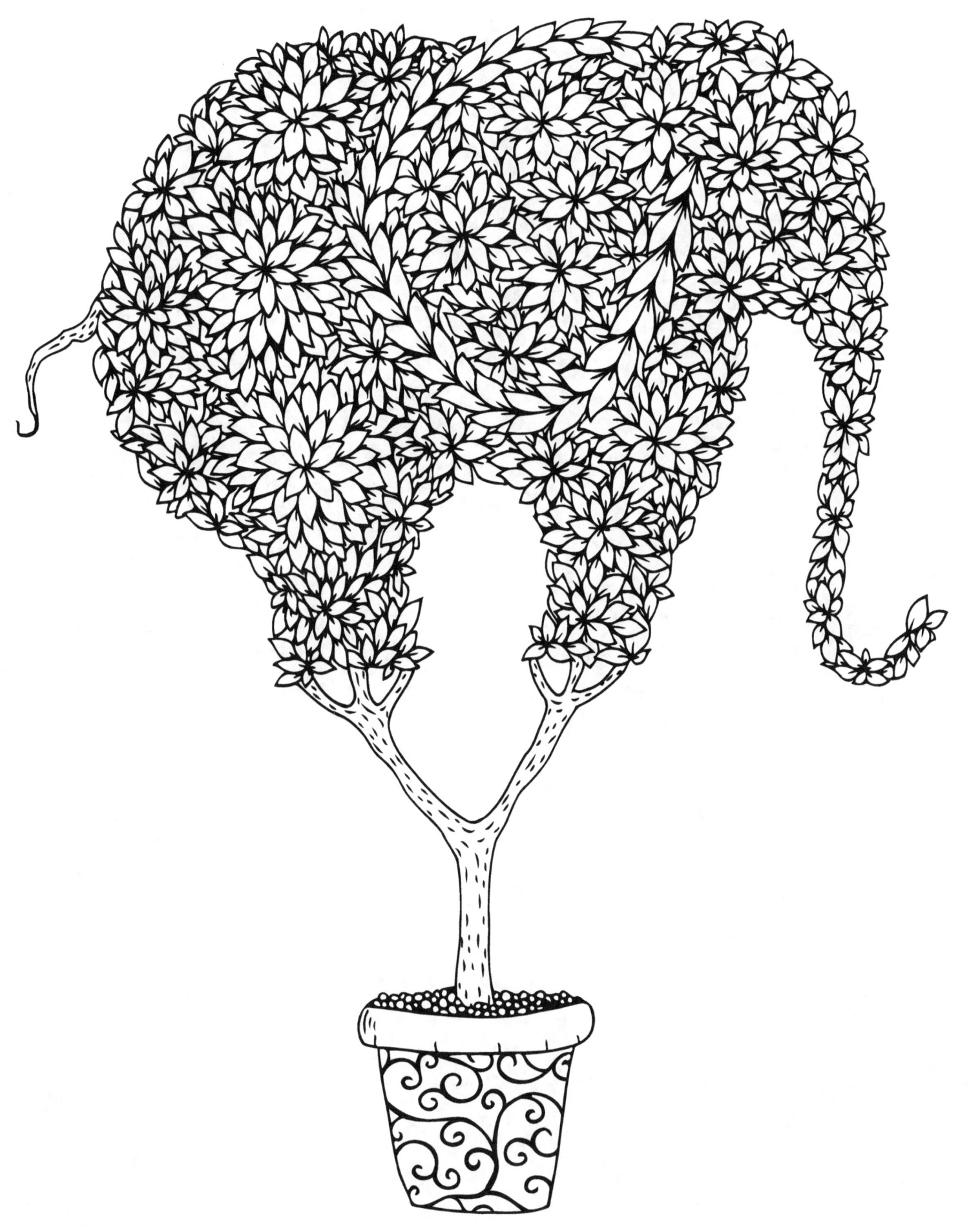

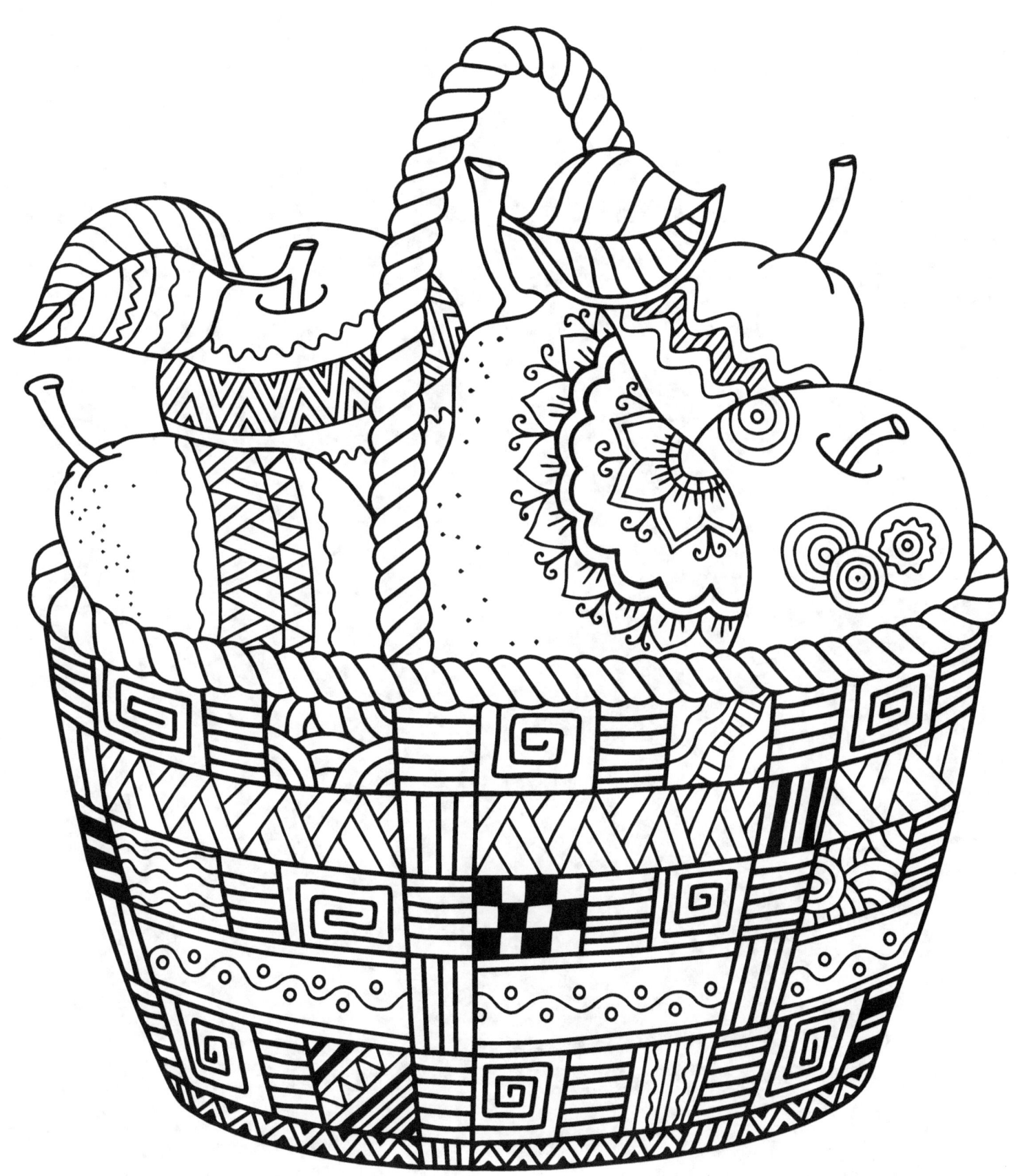

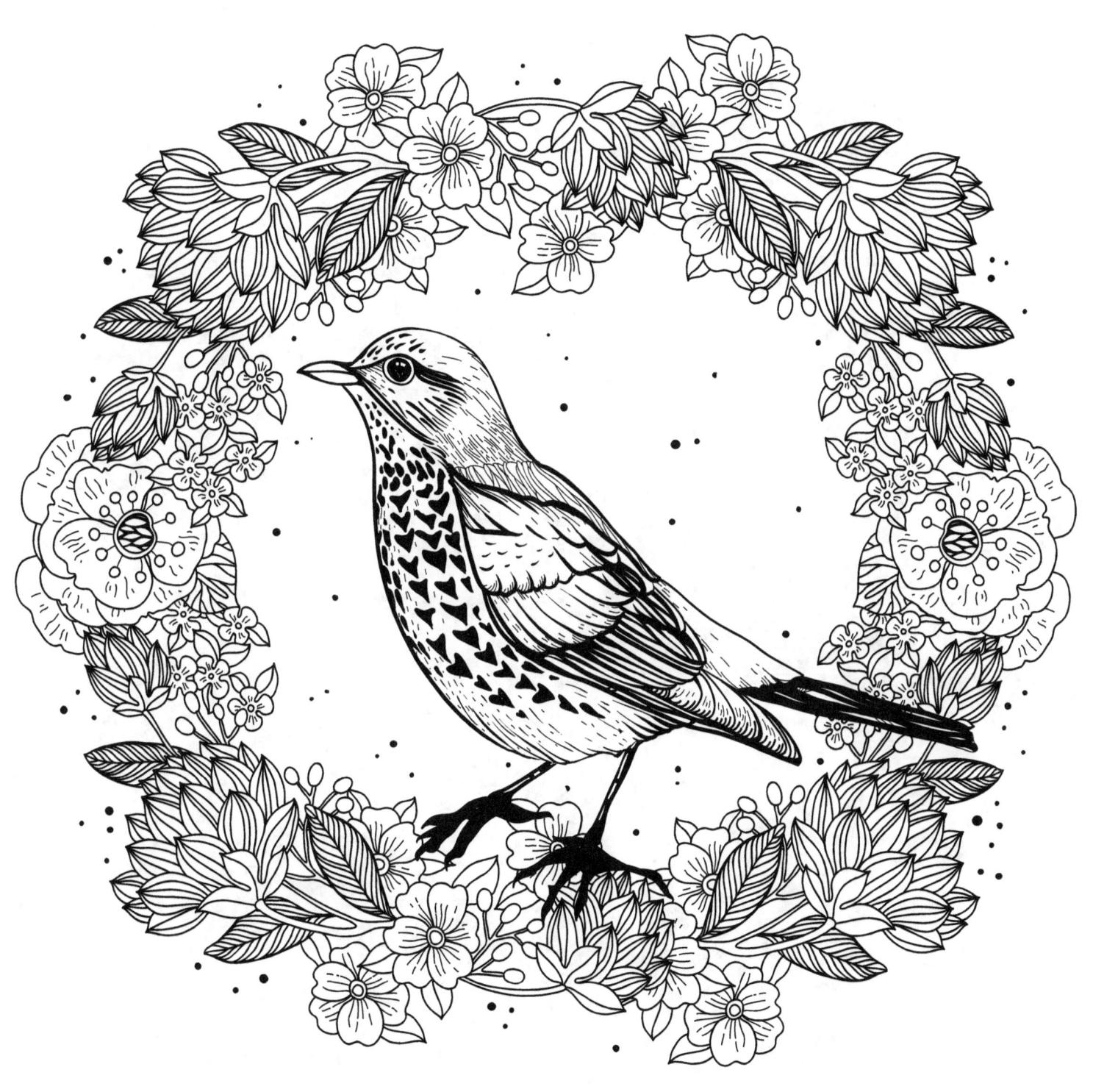

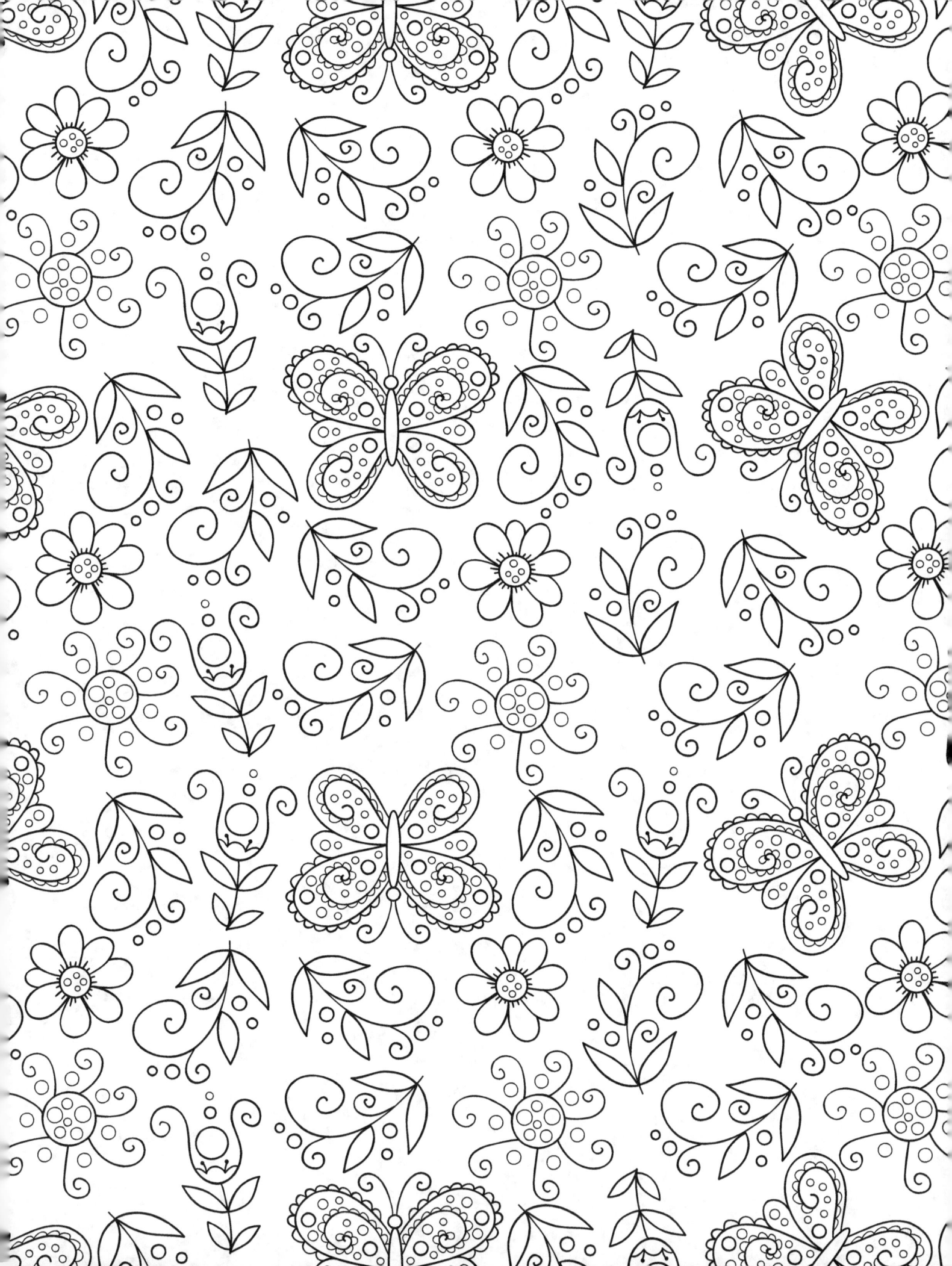

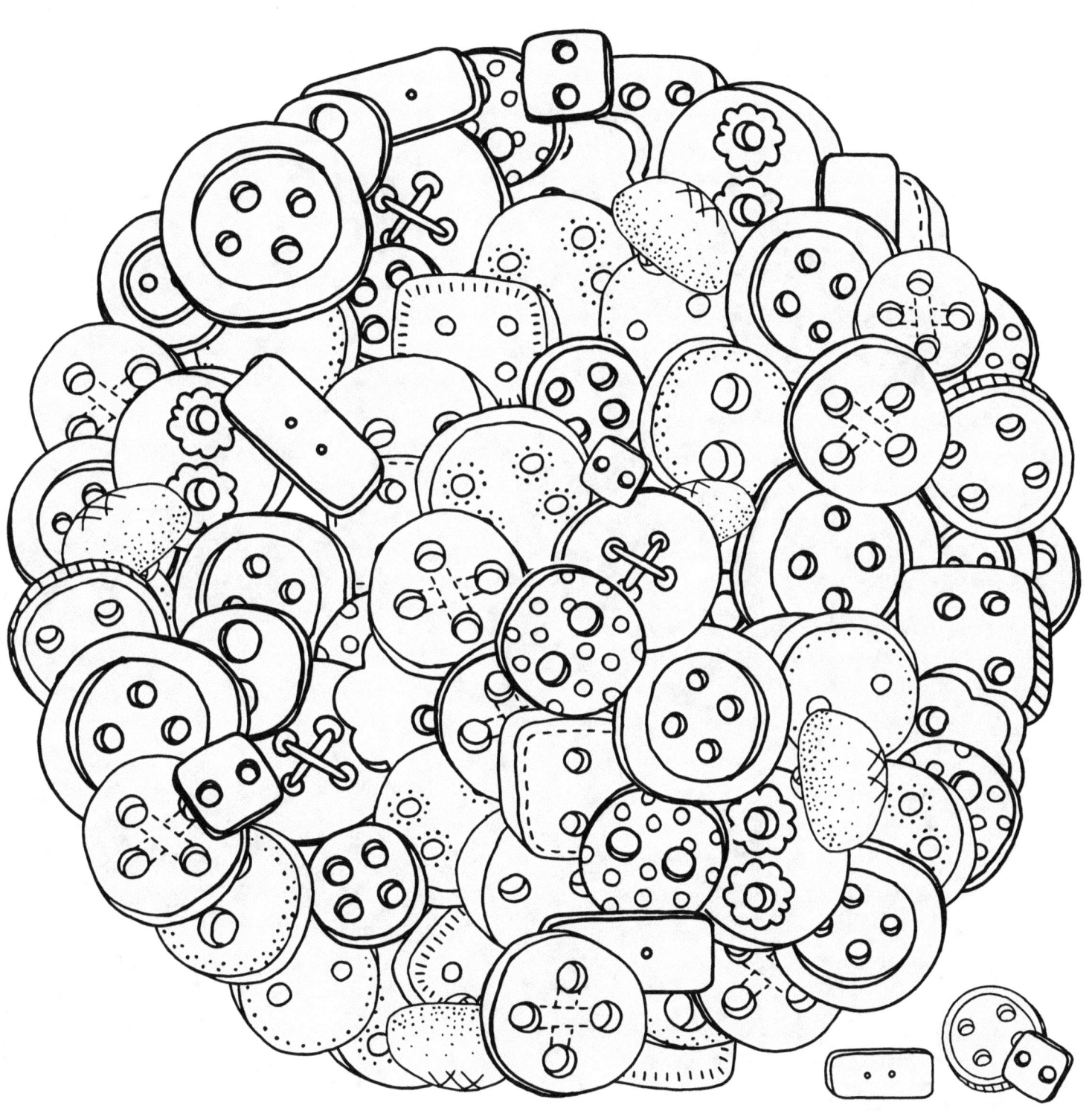

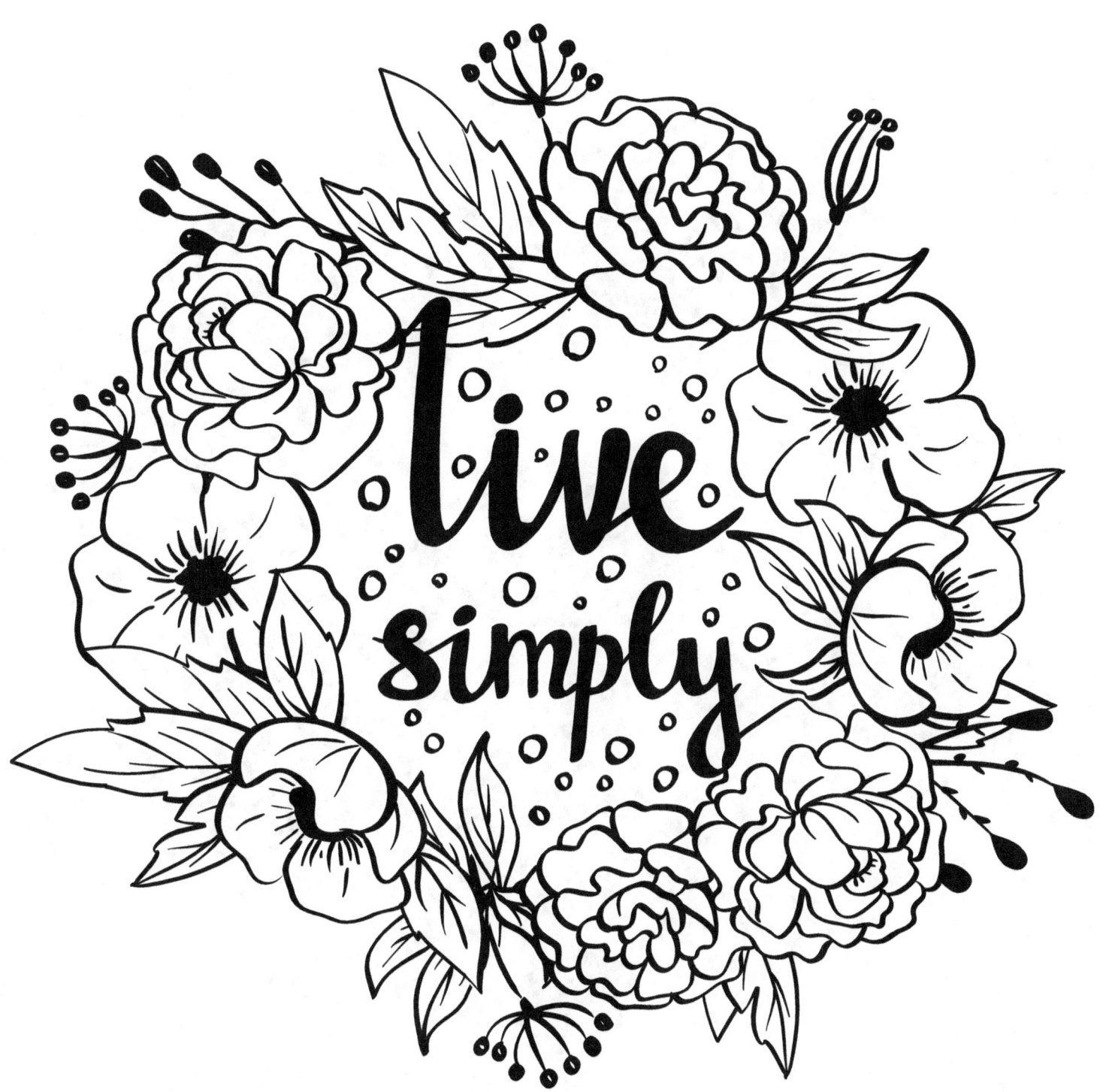

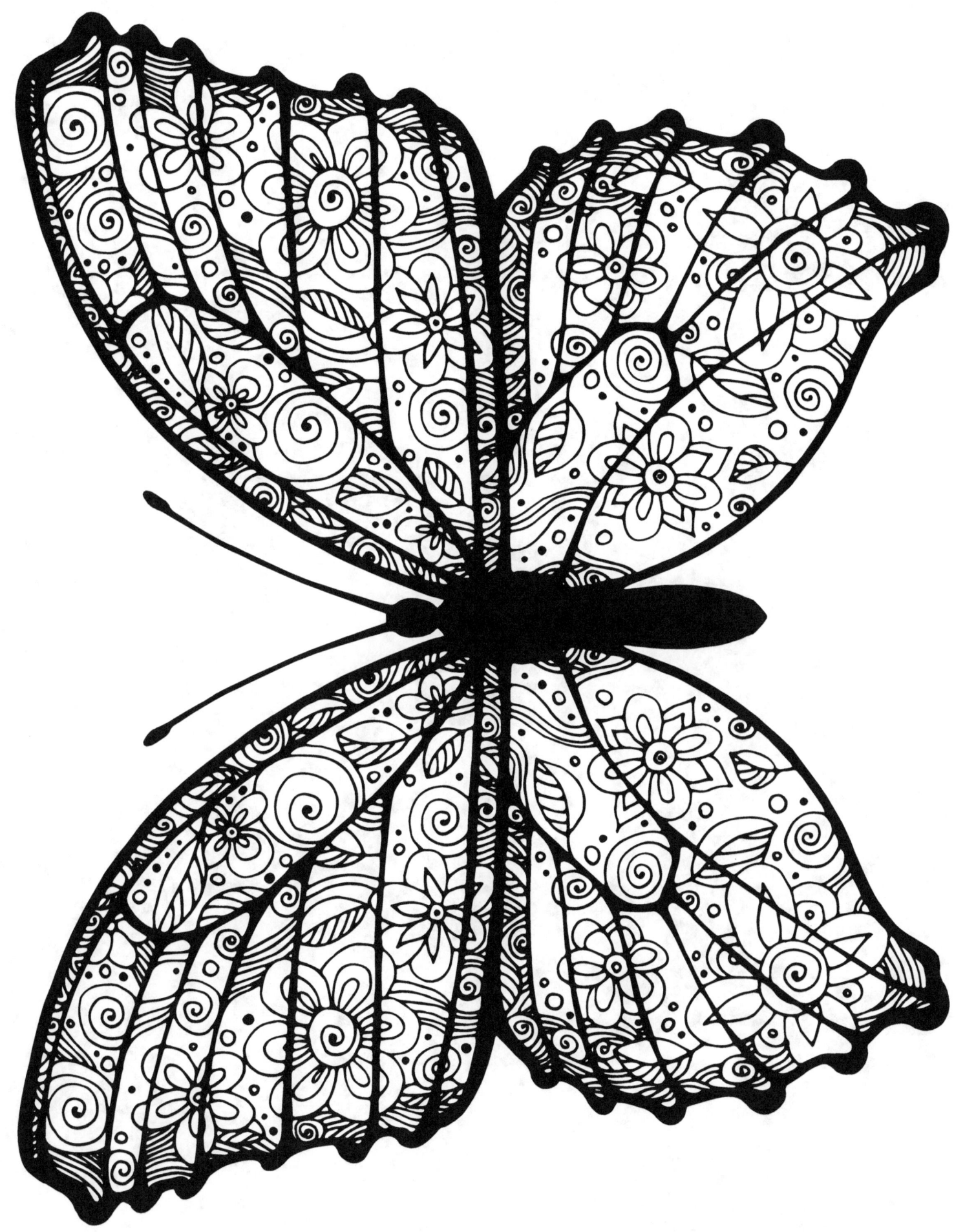

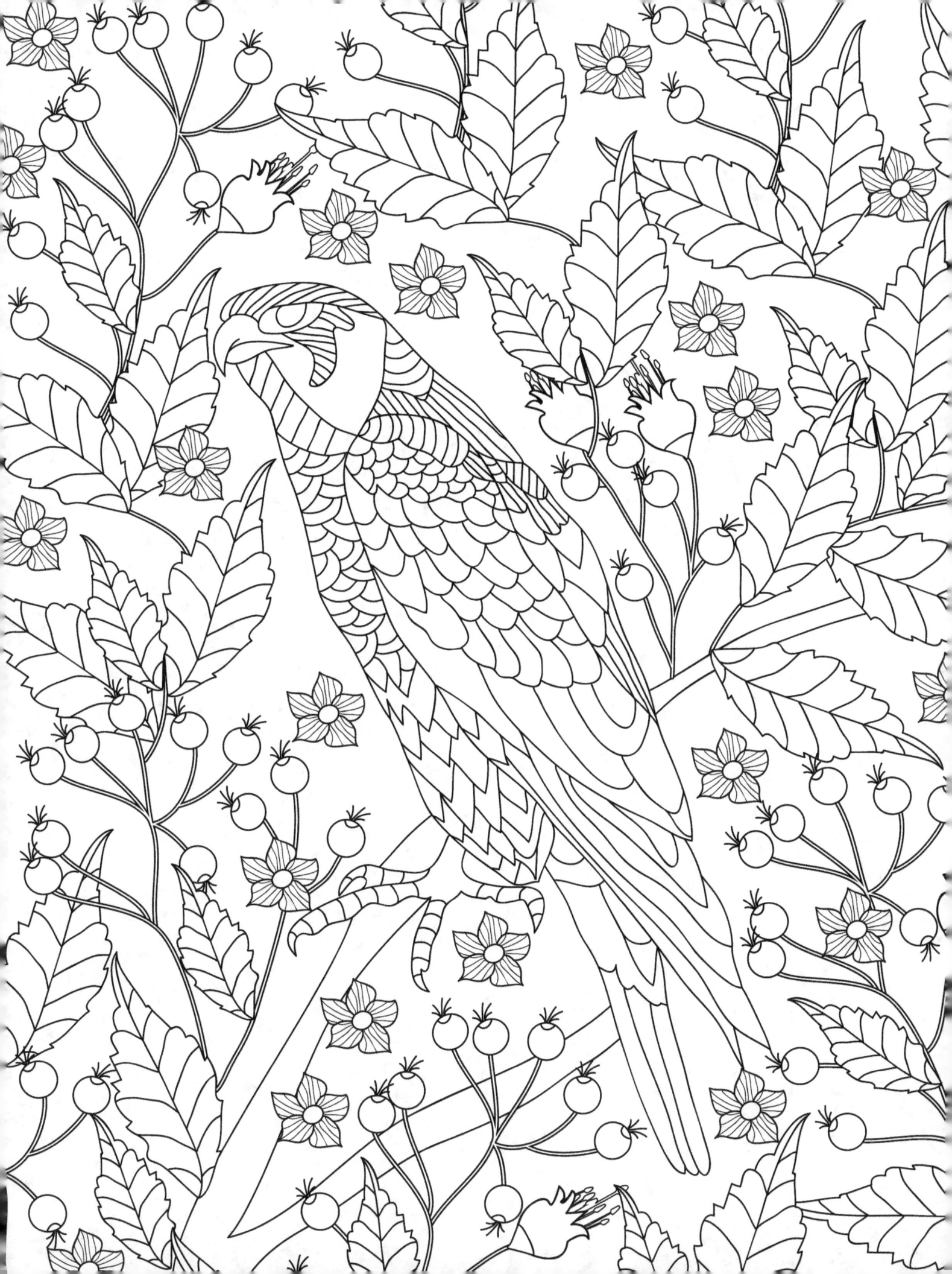

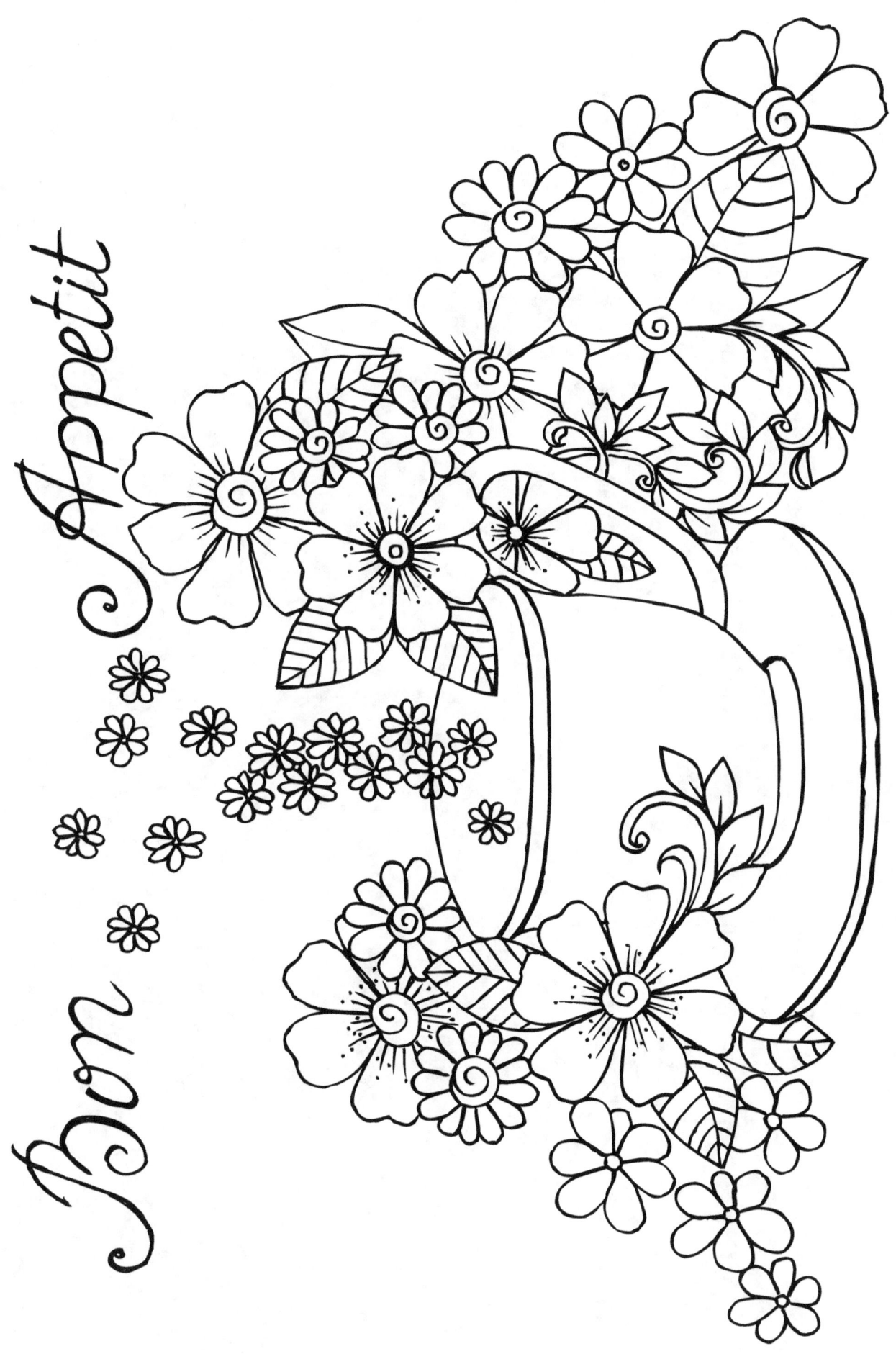

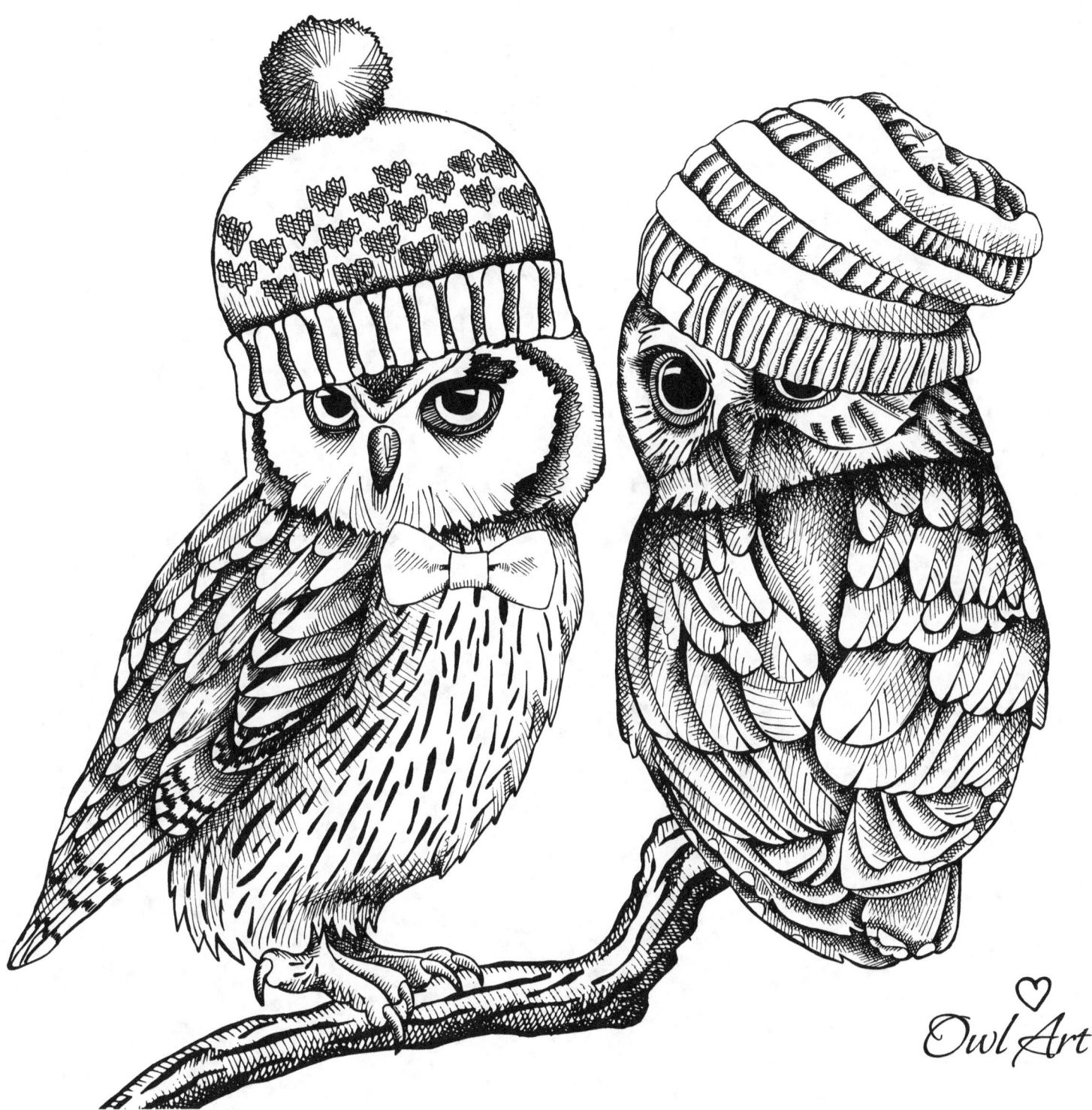

Owl♡Art

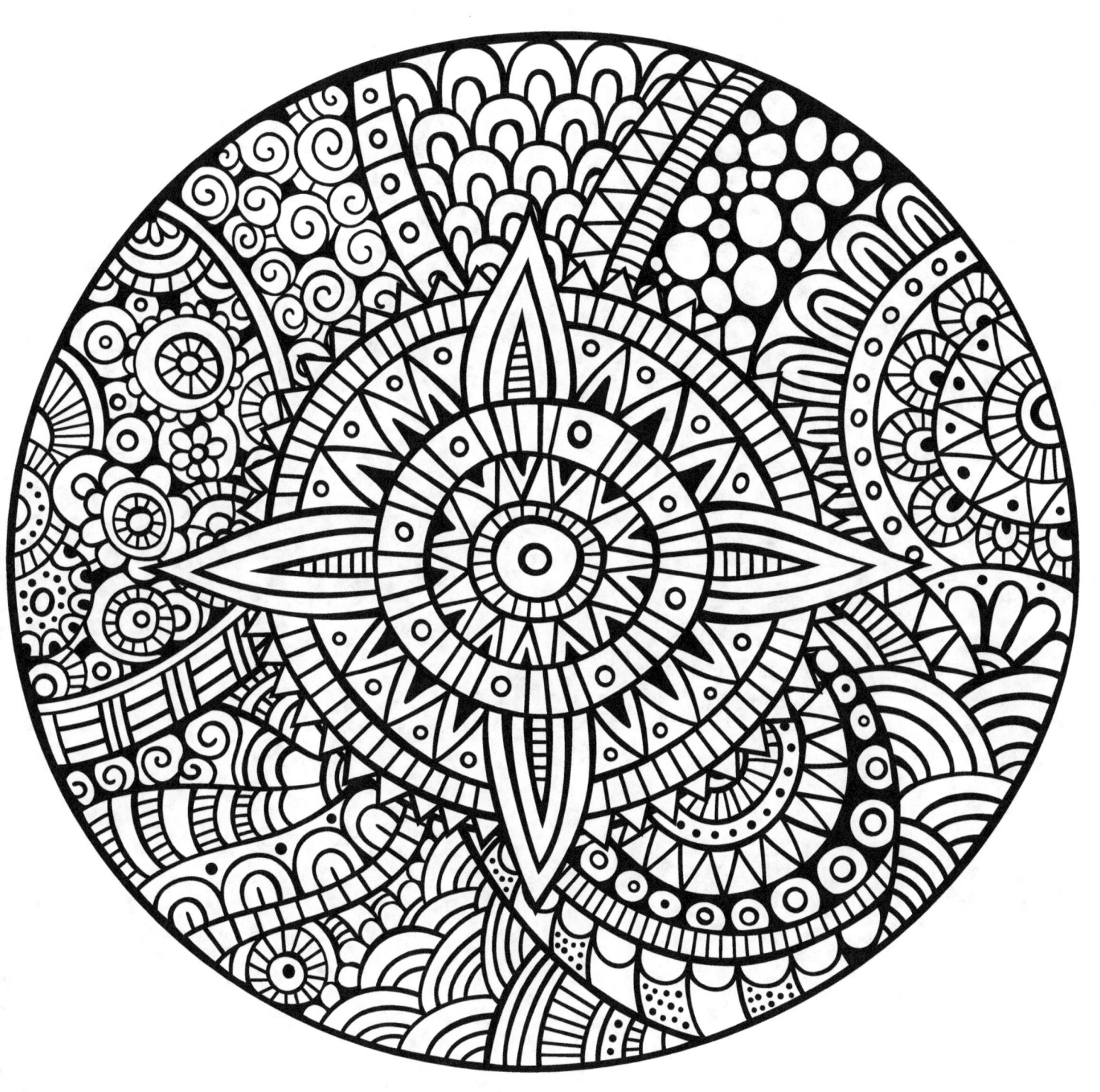

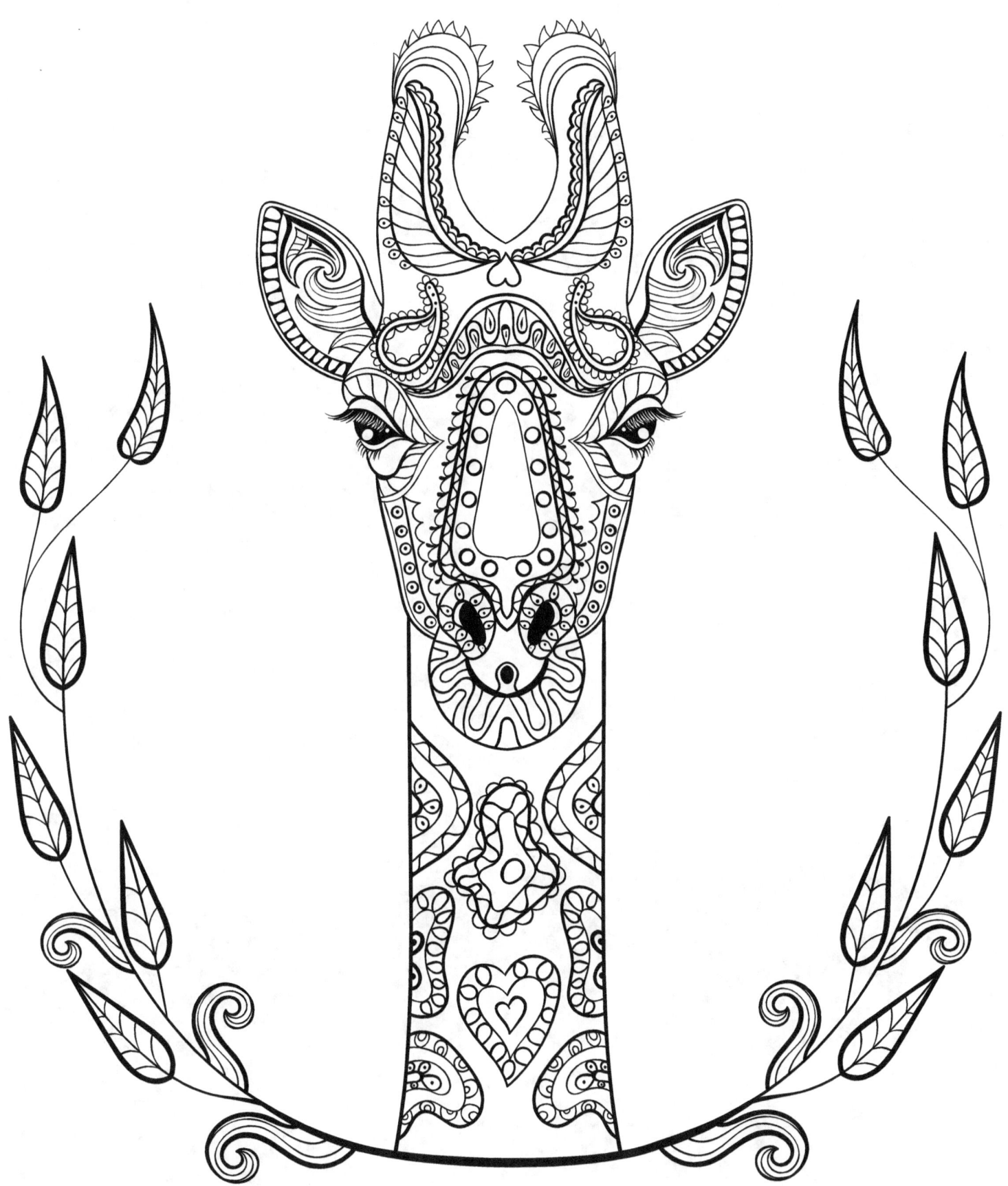

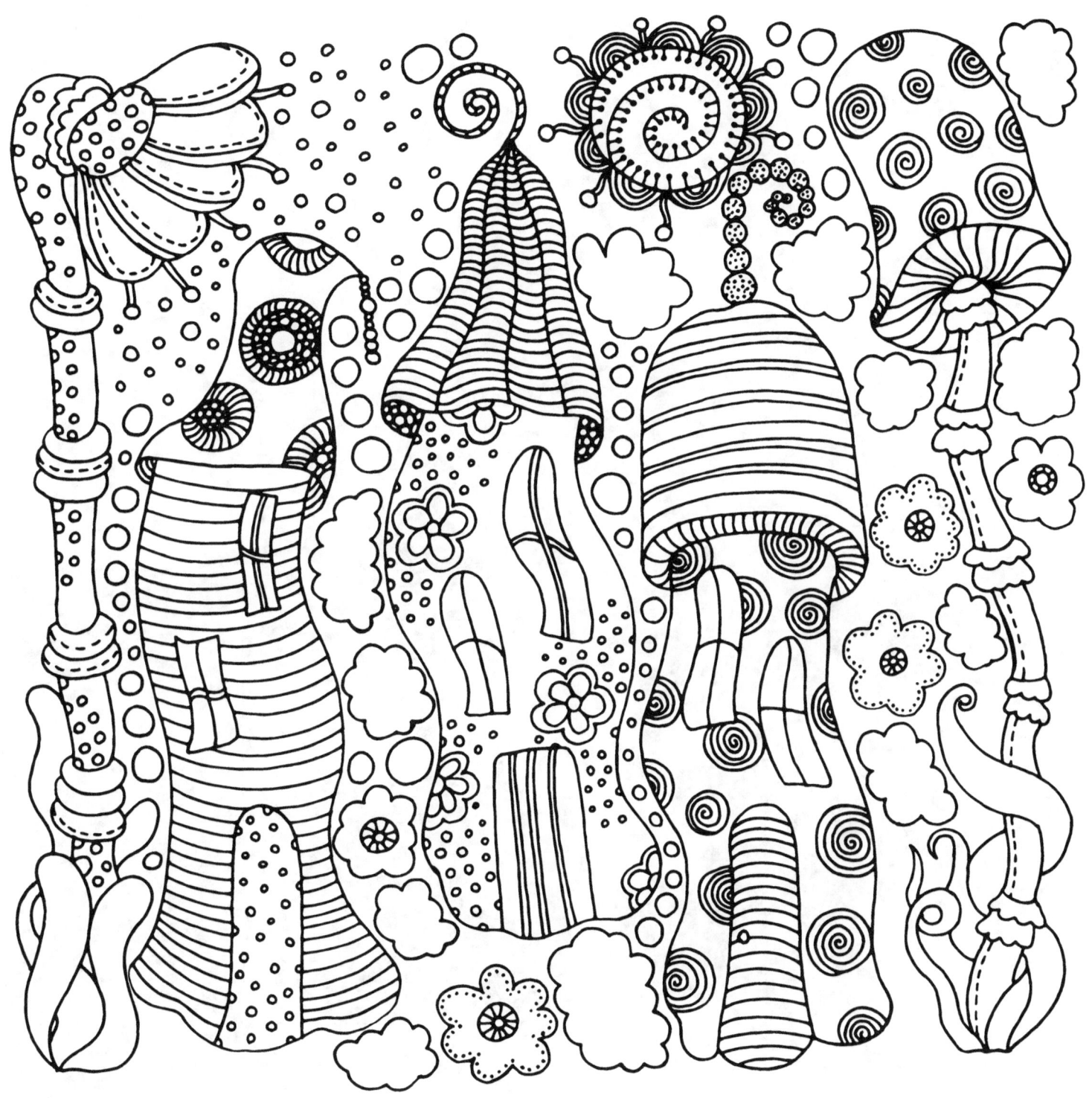

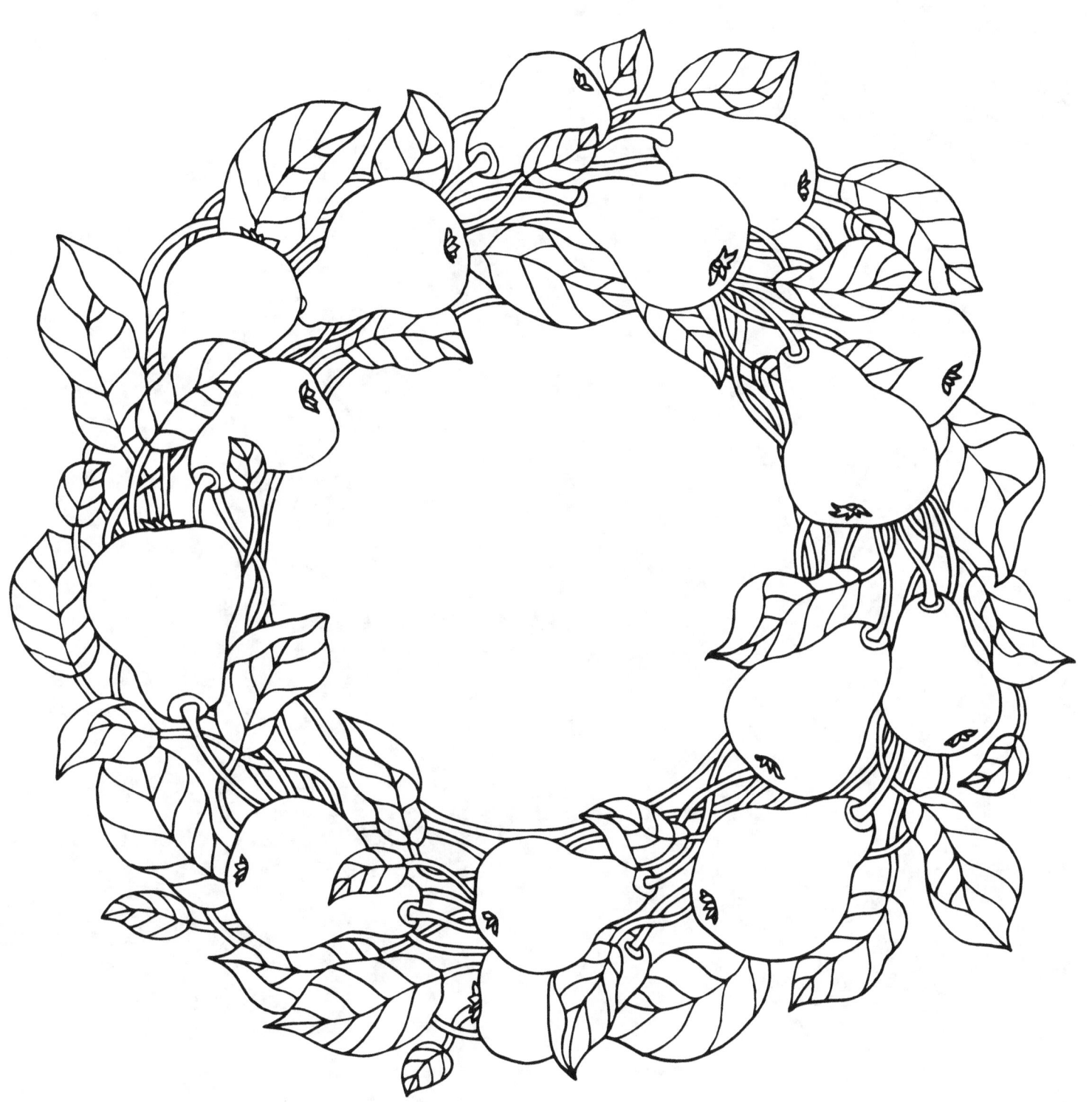

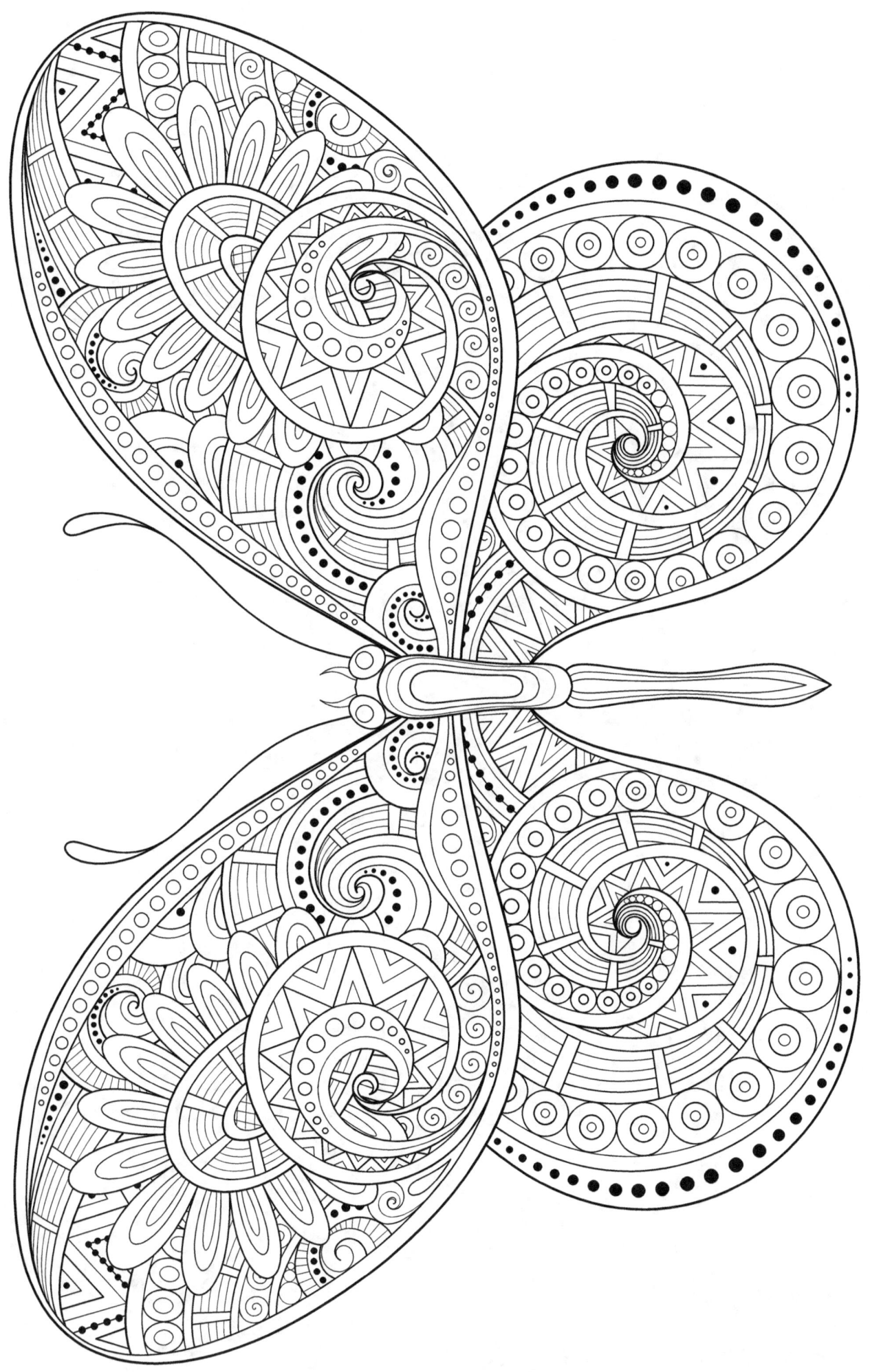

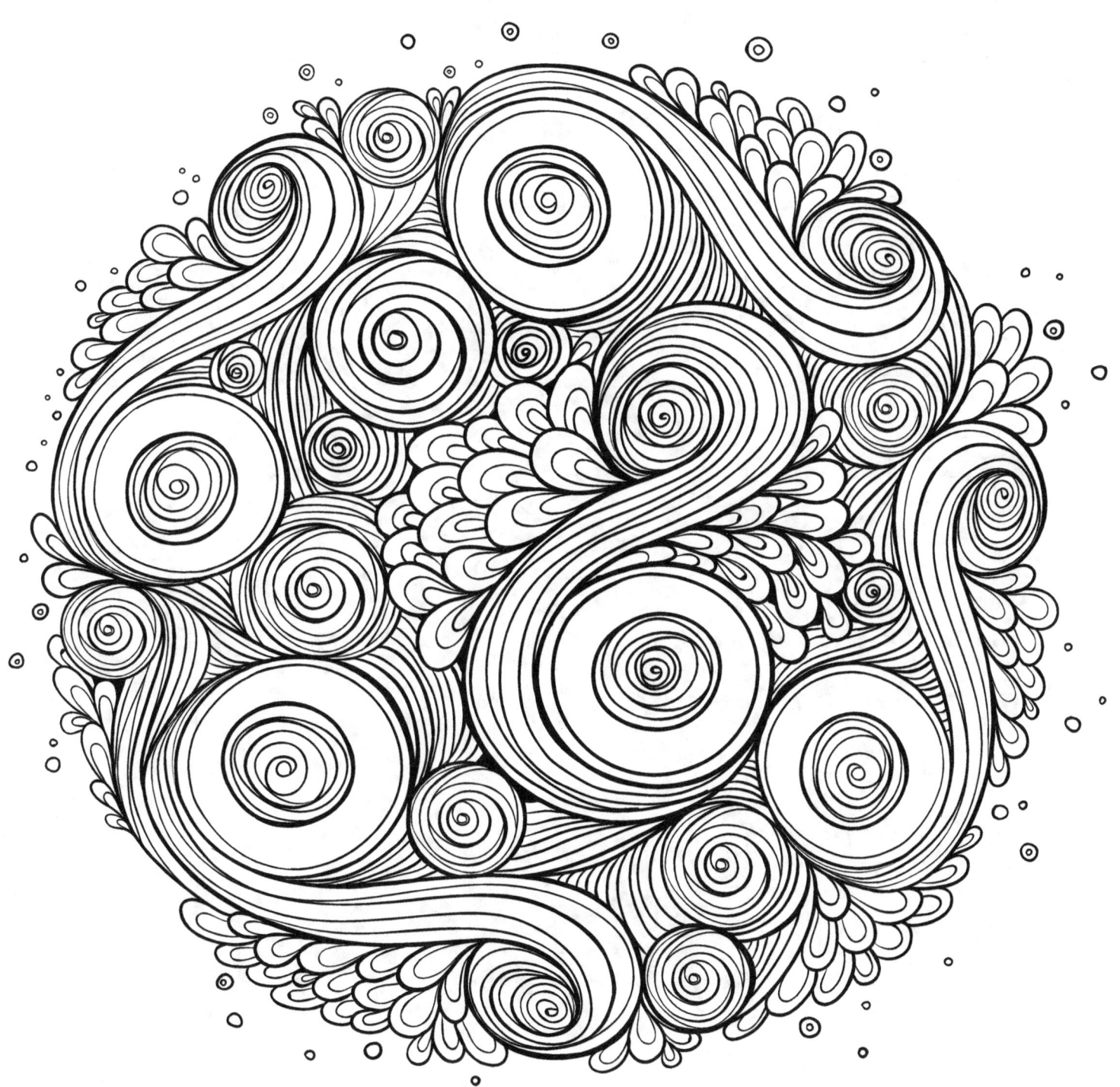

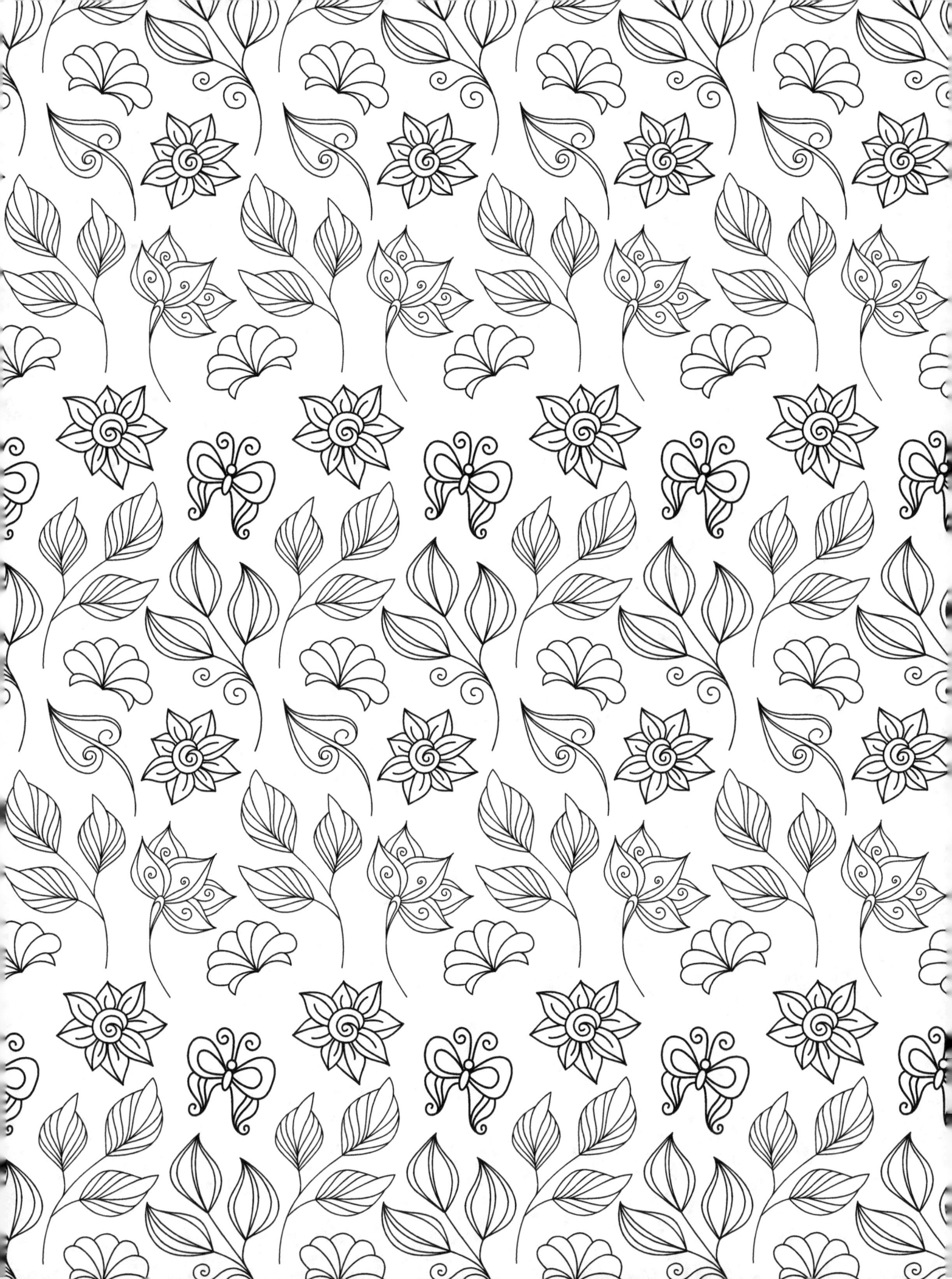

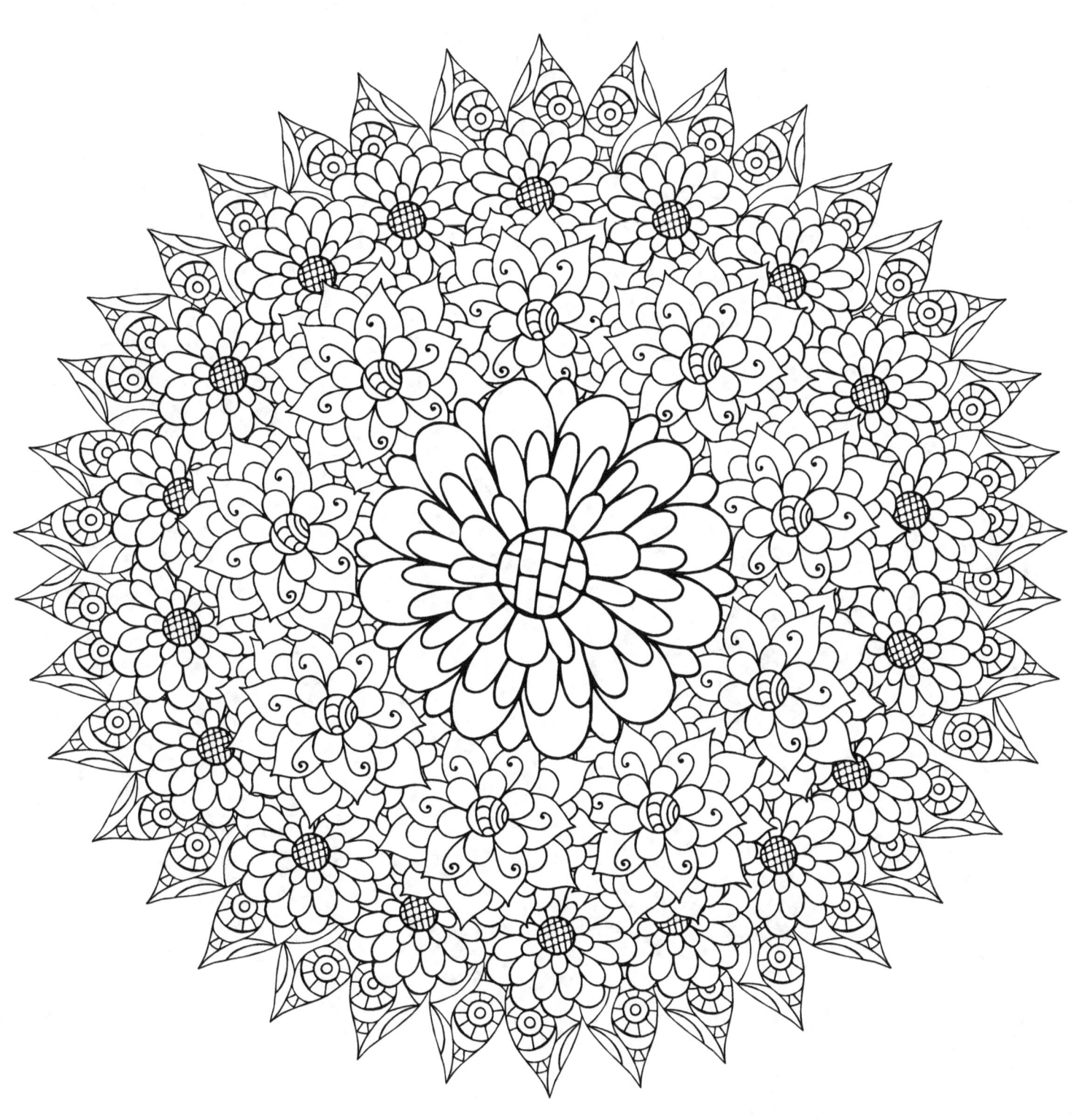

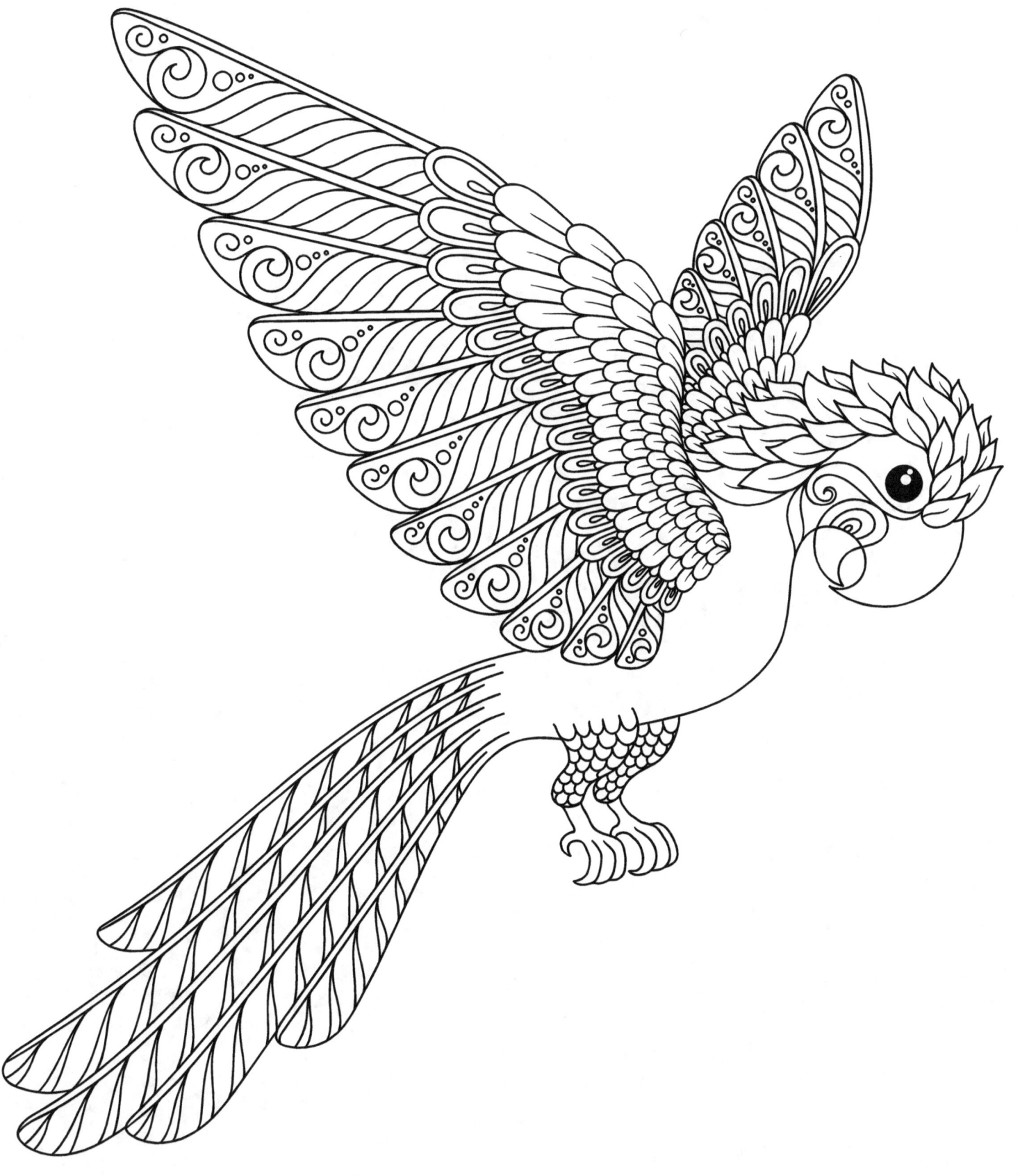

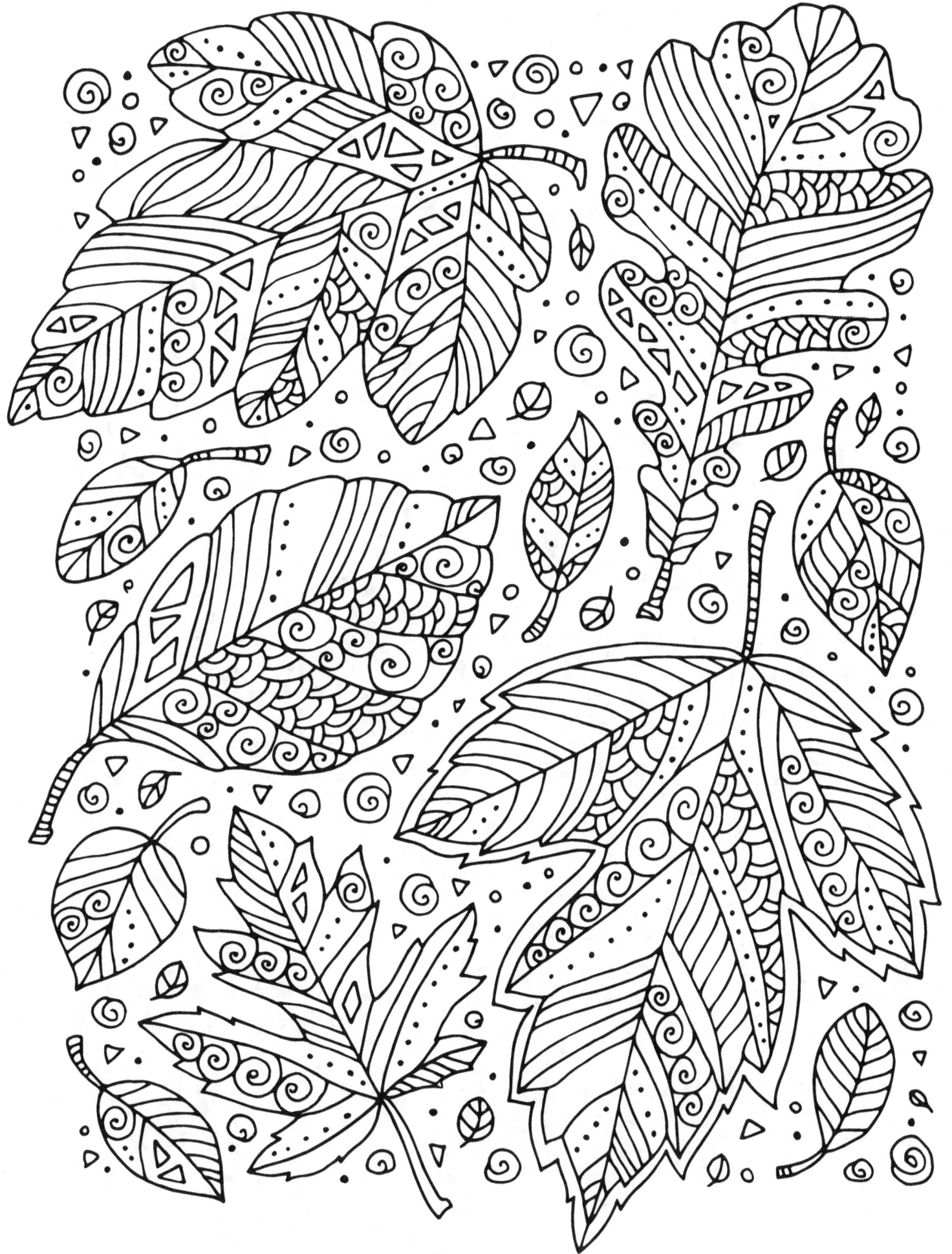

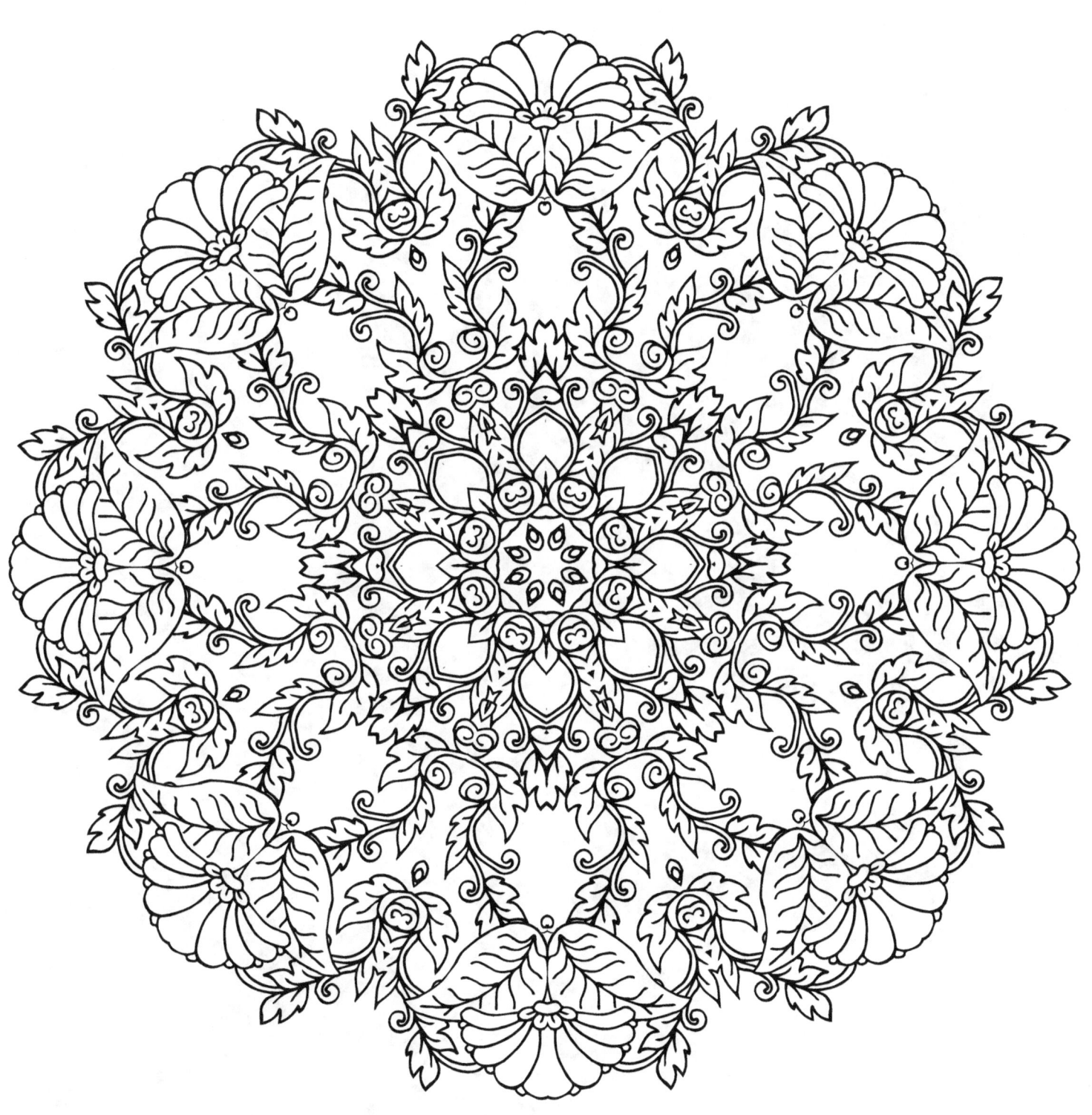

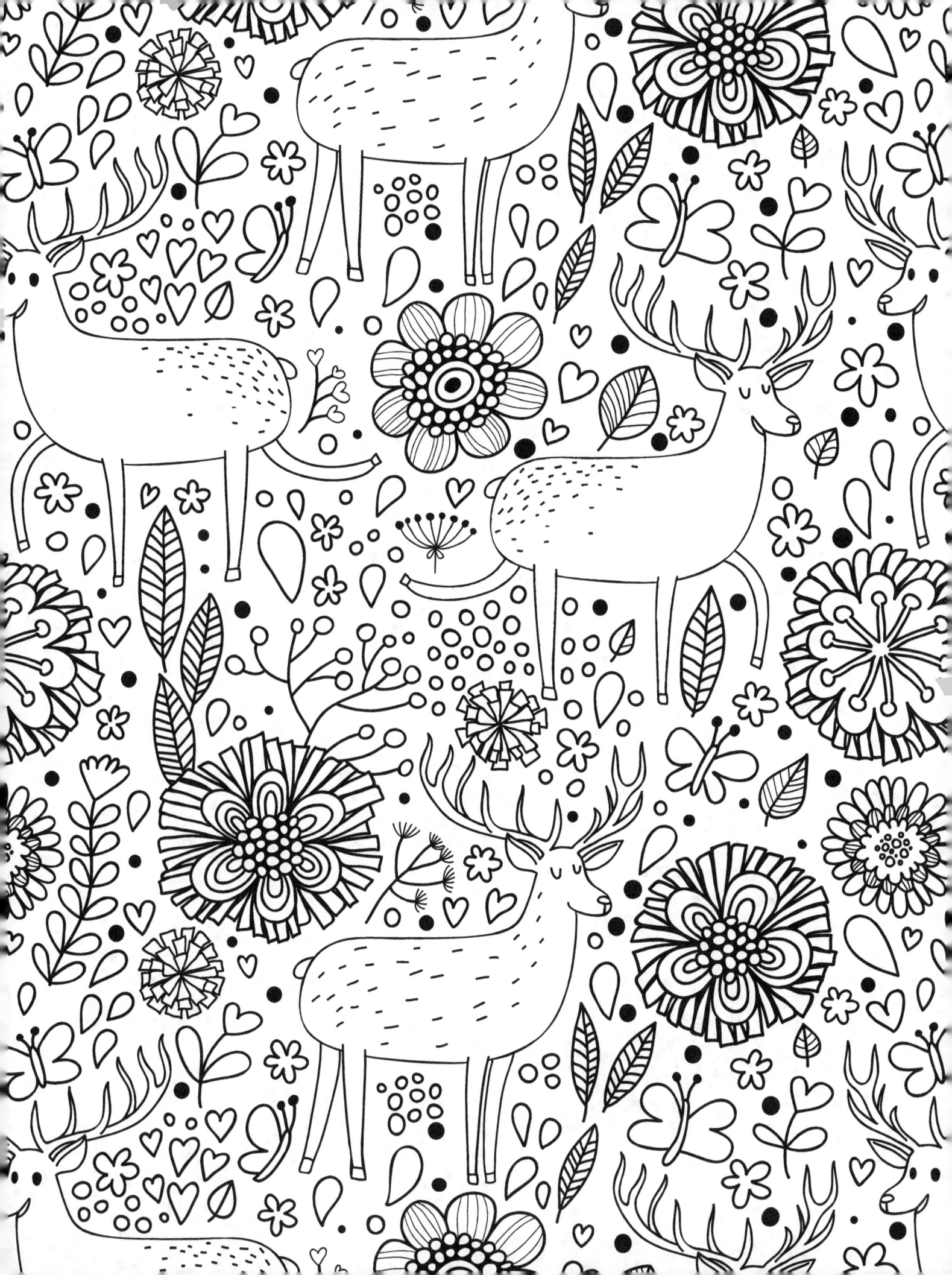

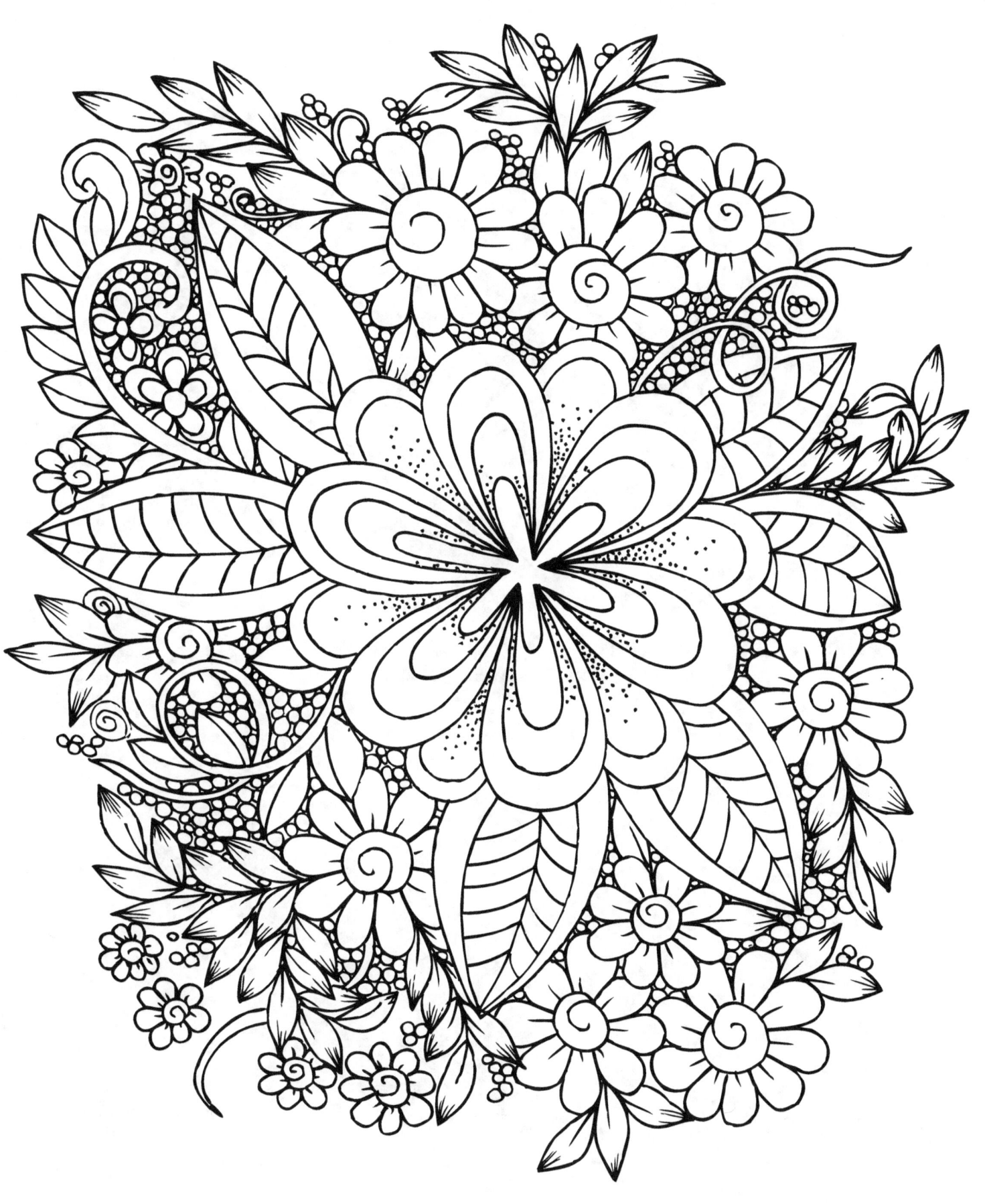

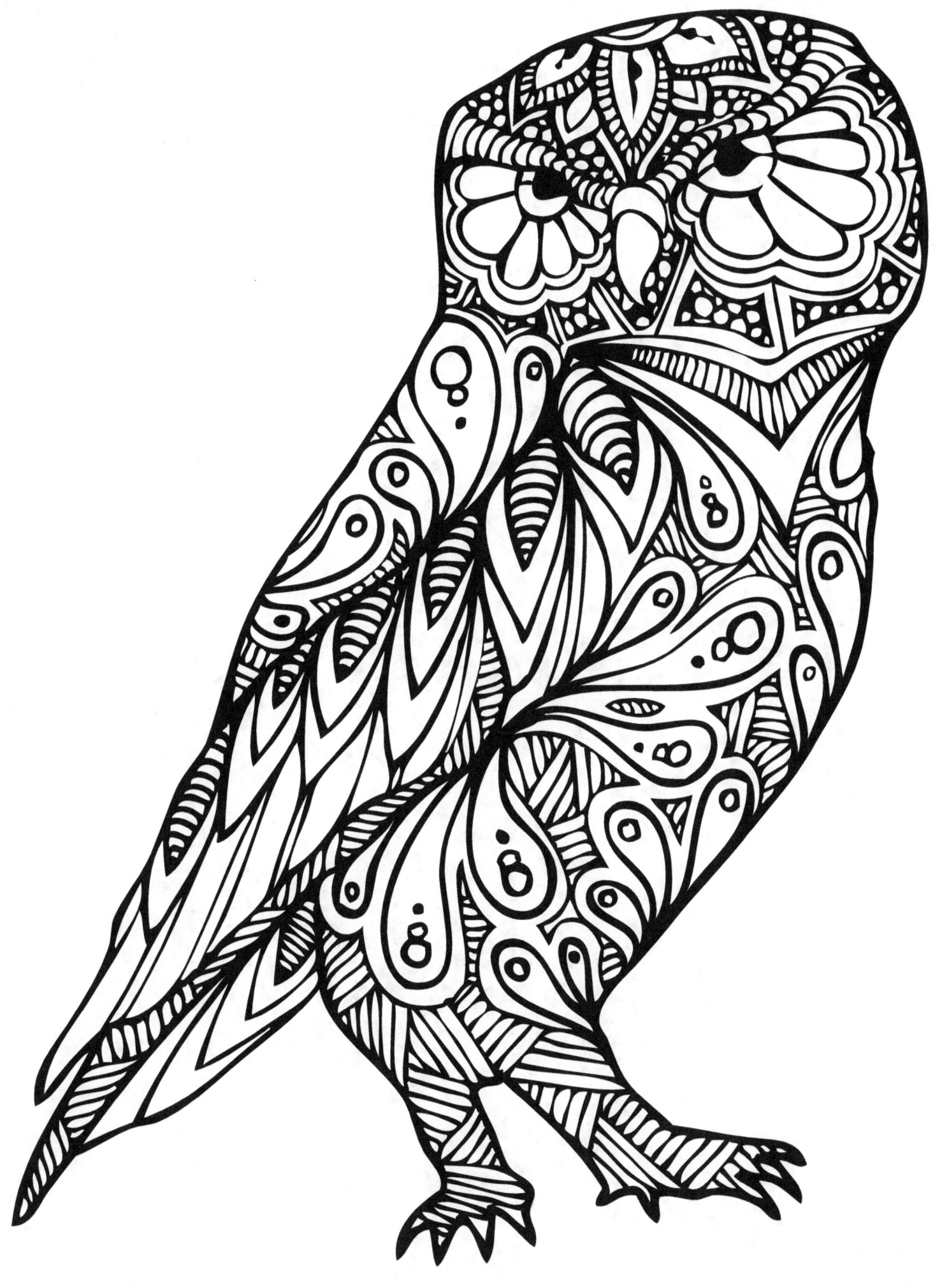

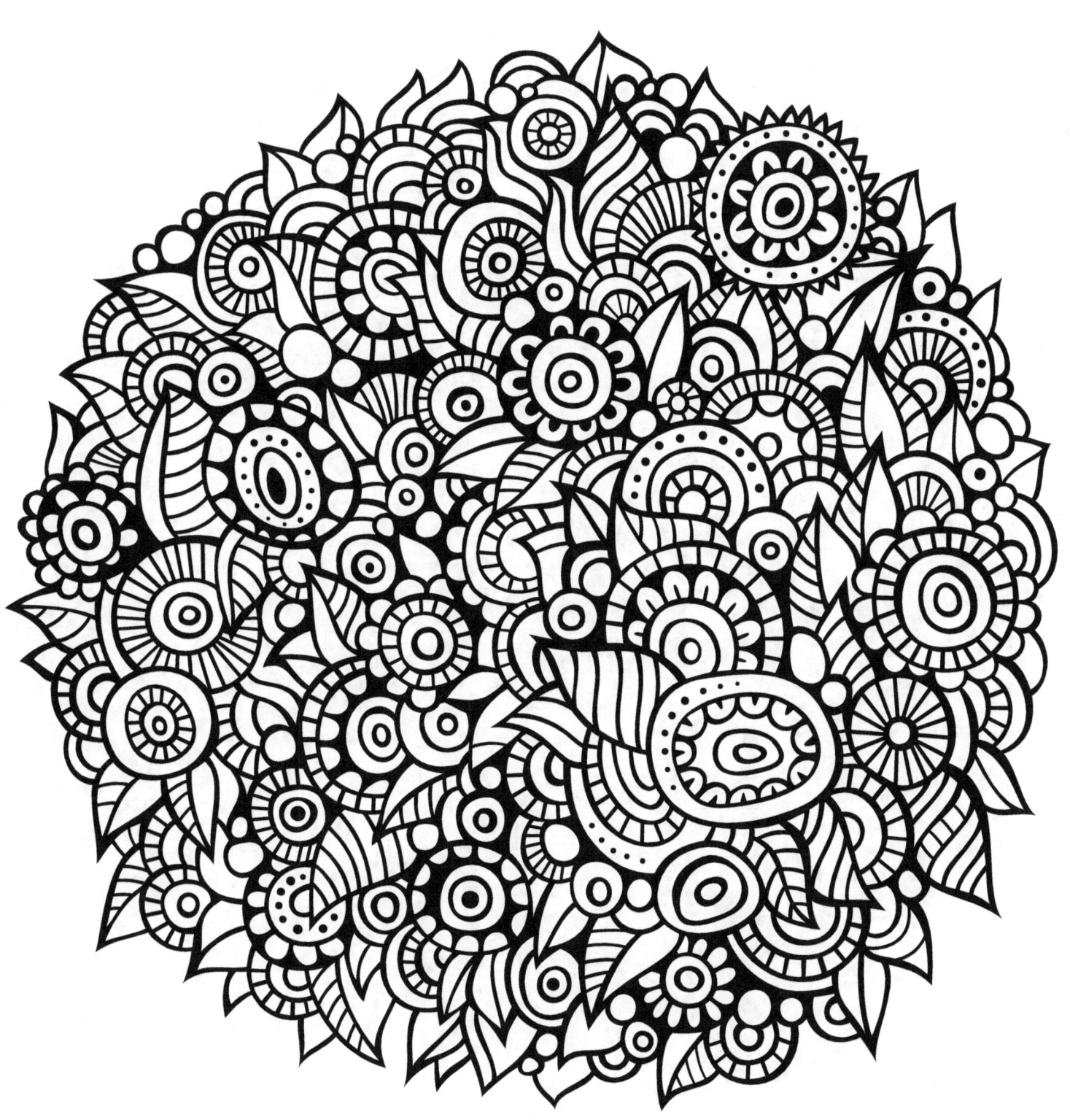

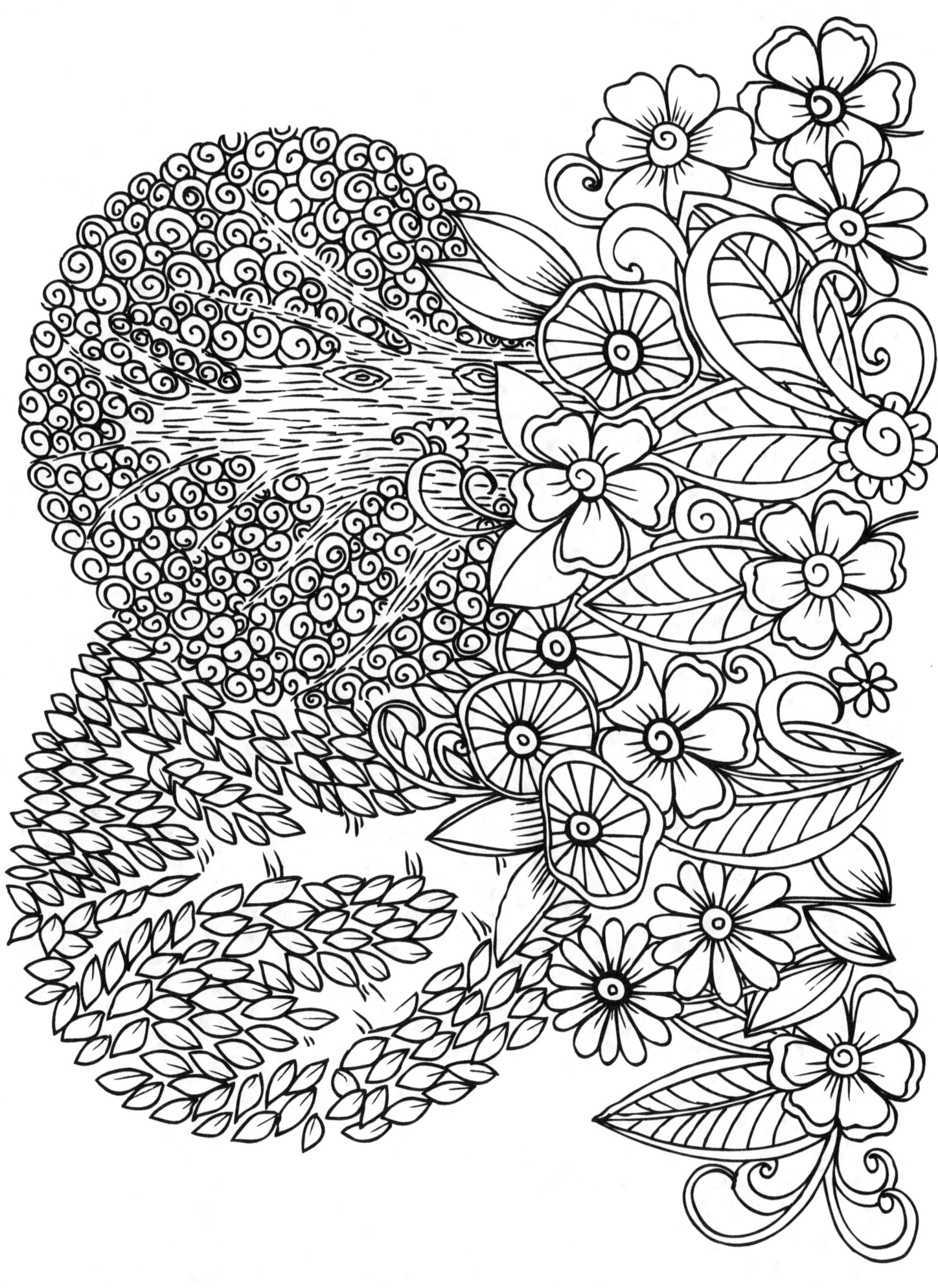

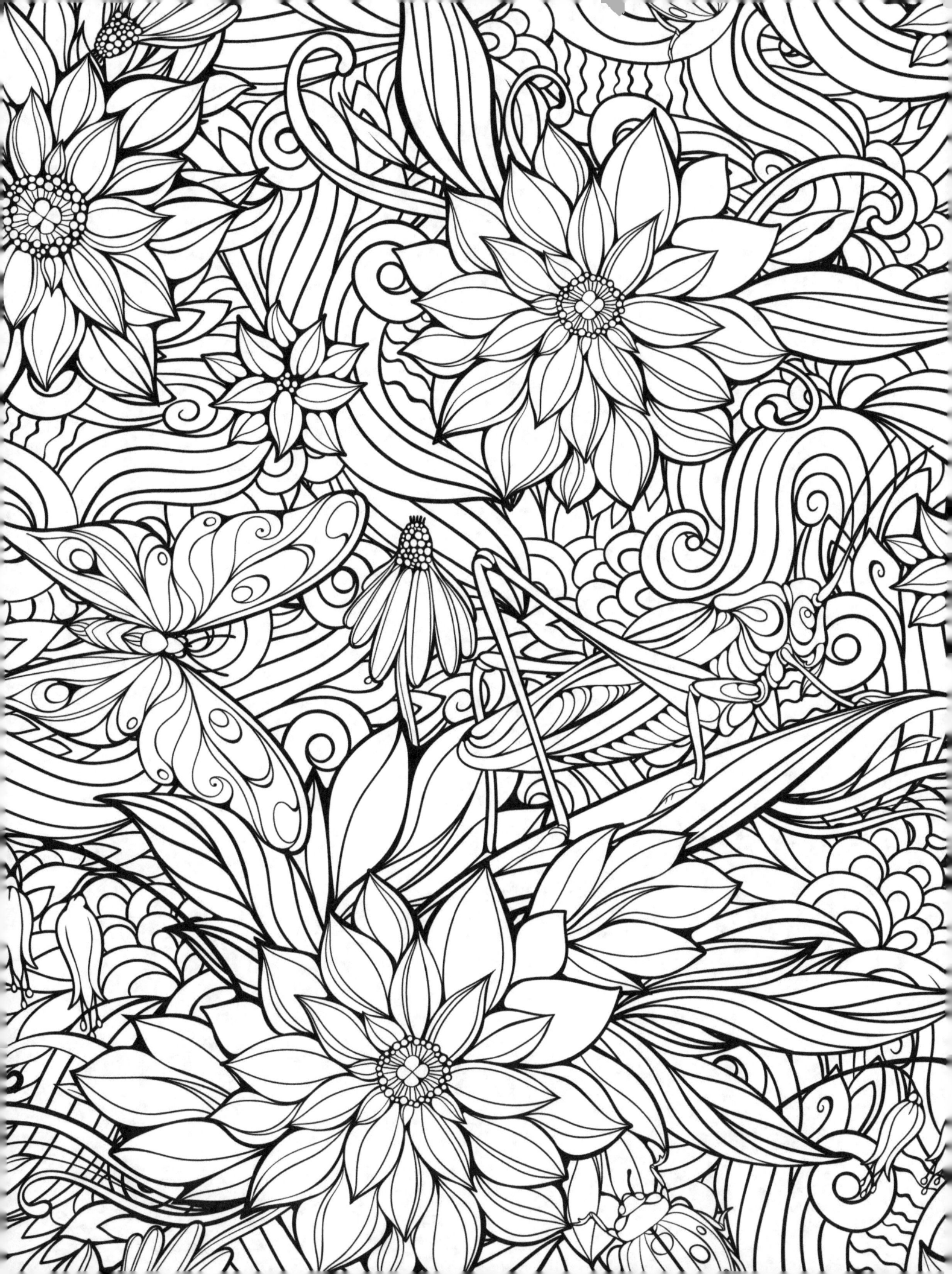

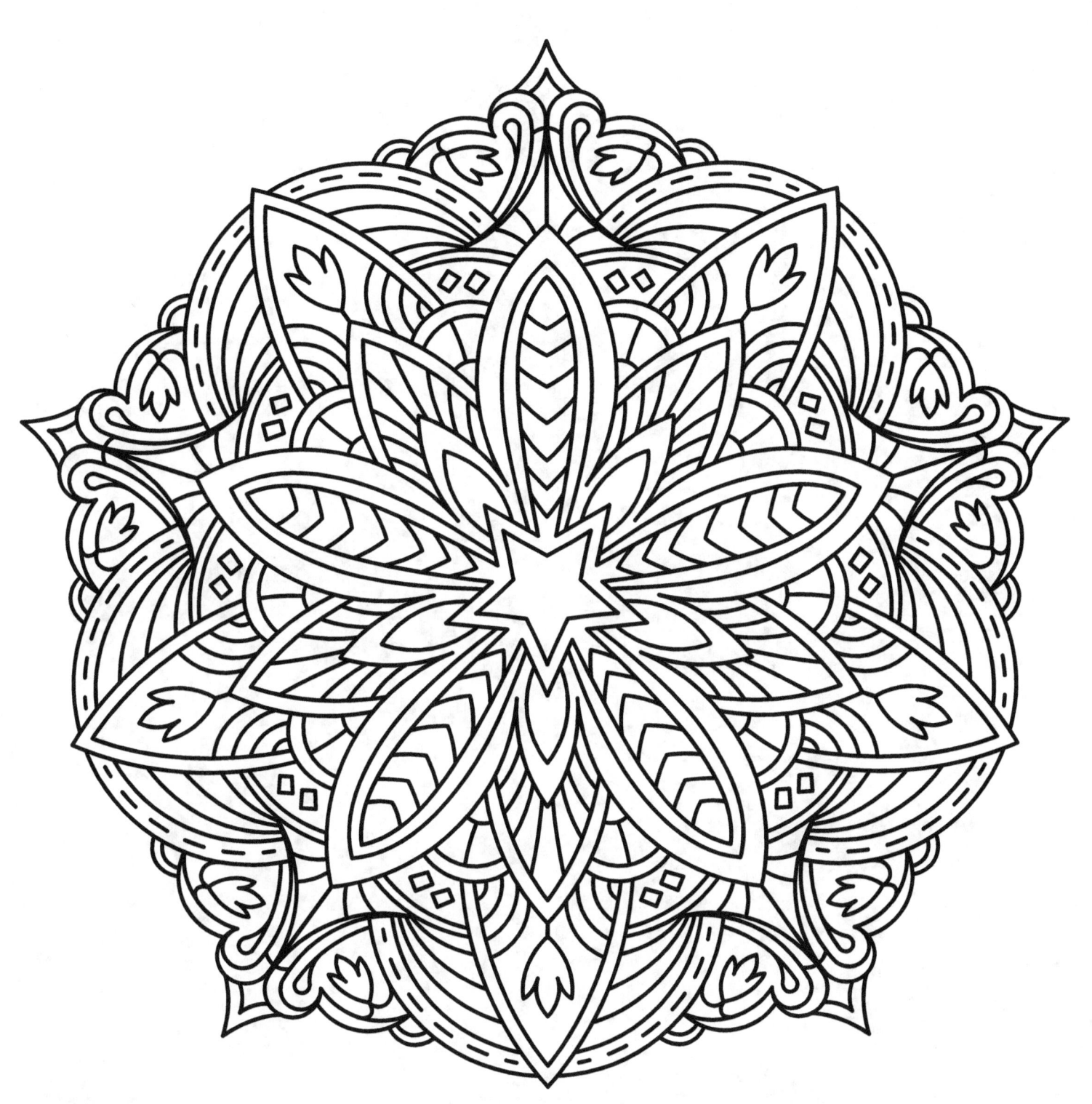

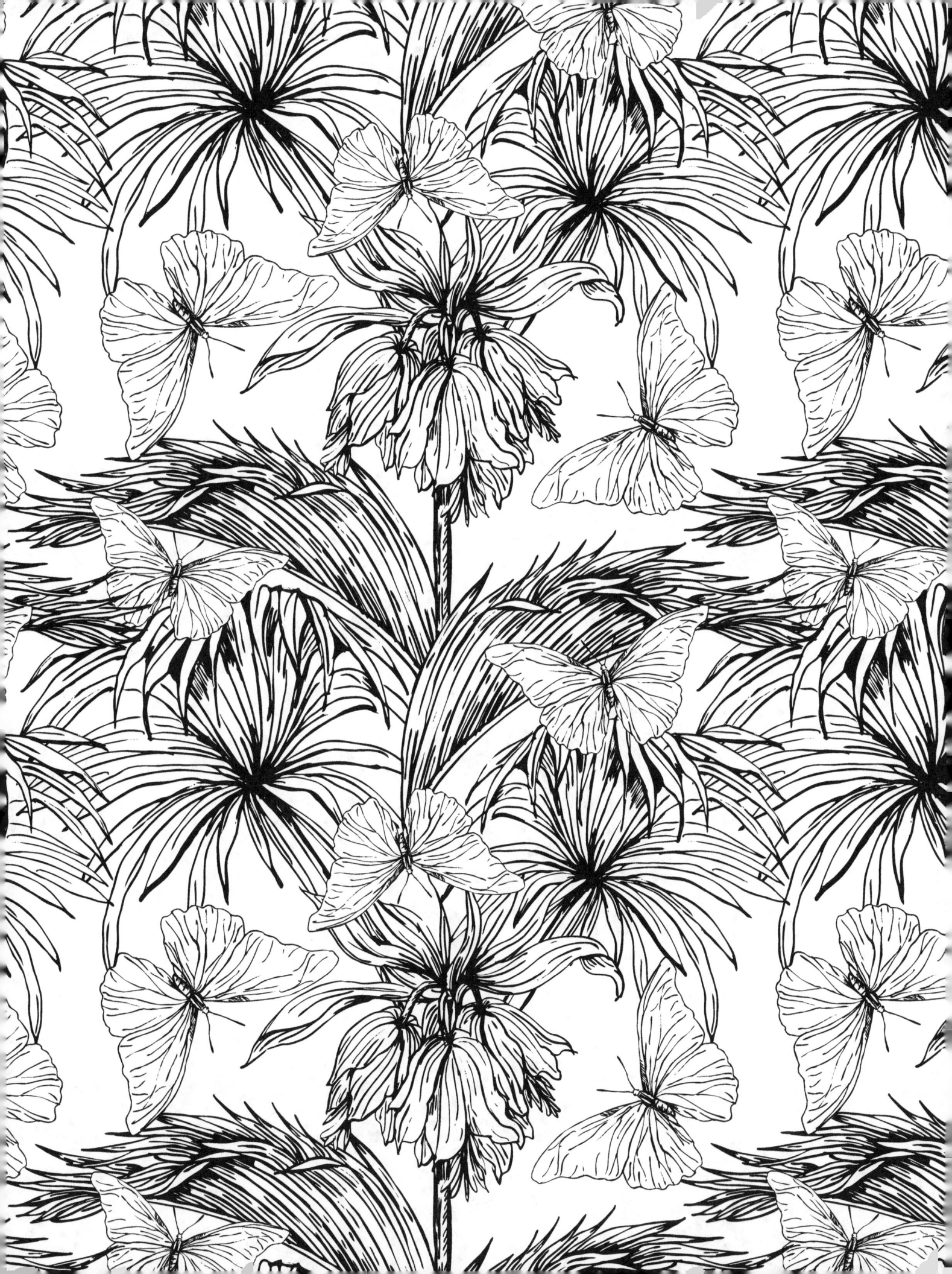

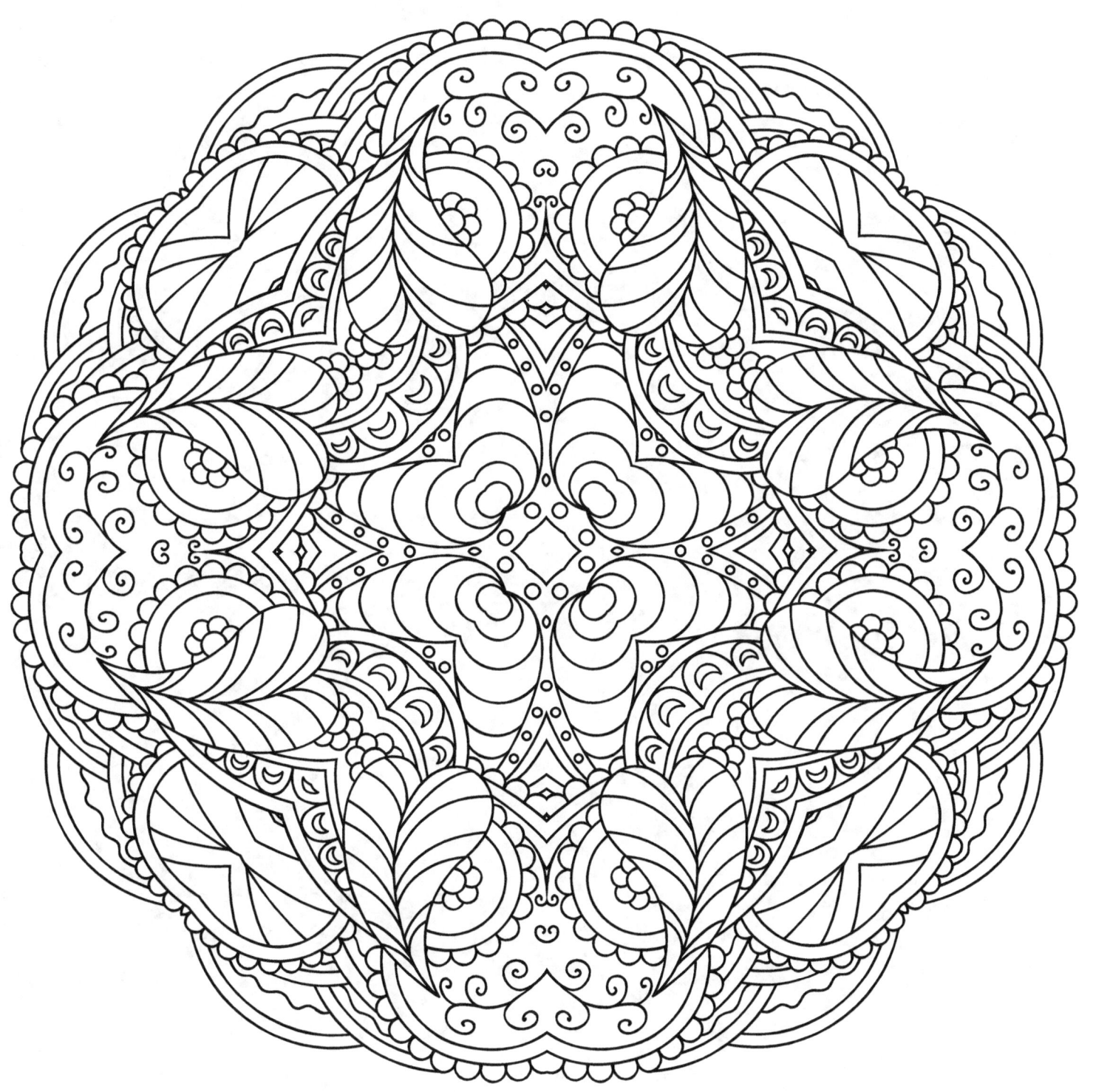

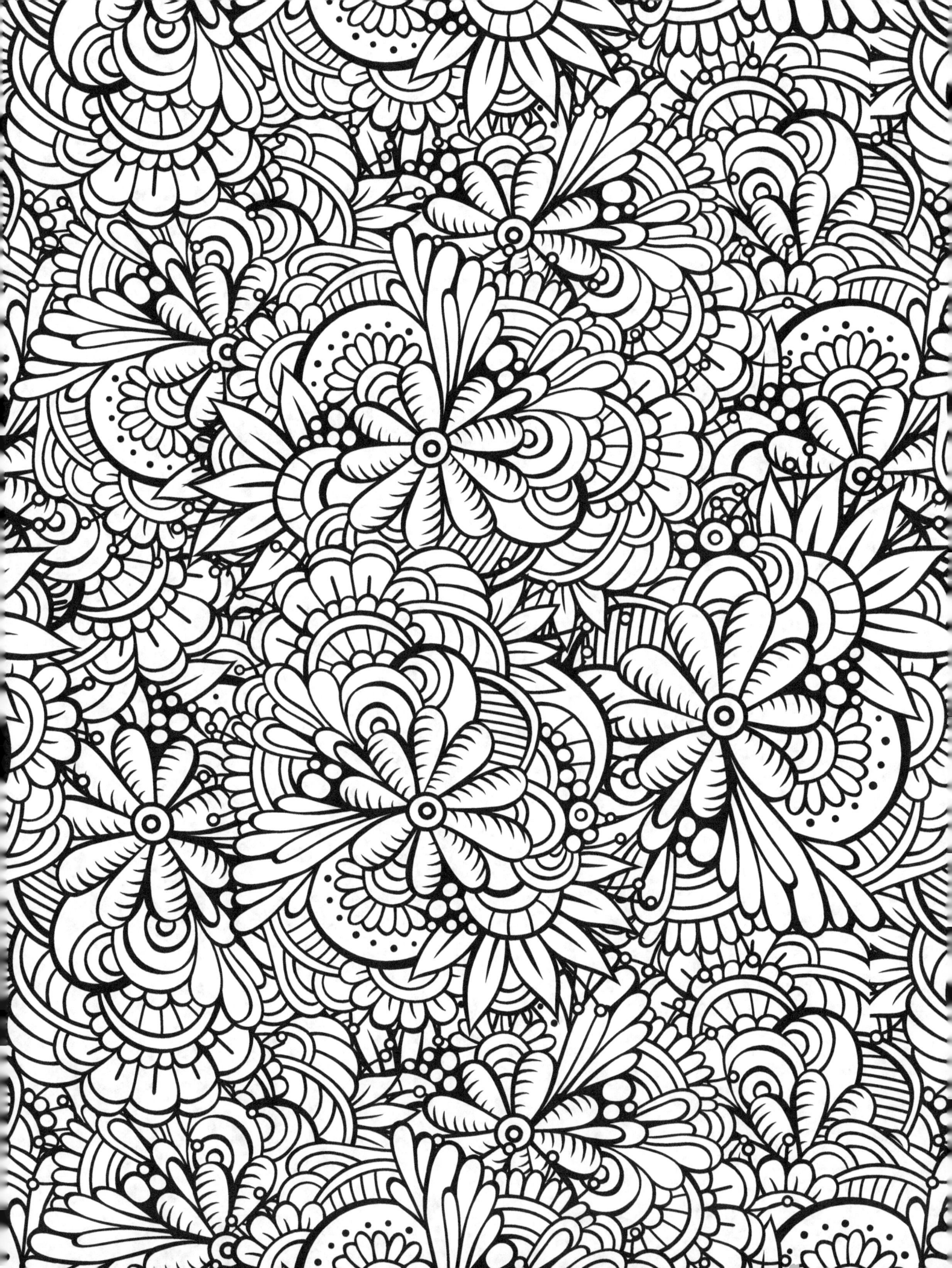

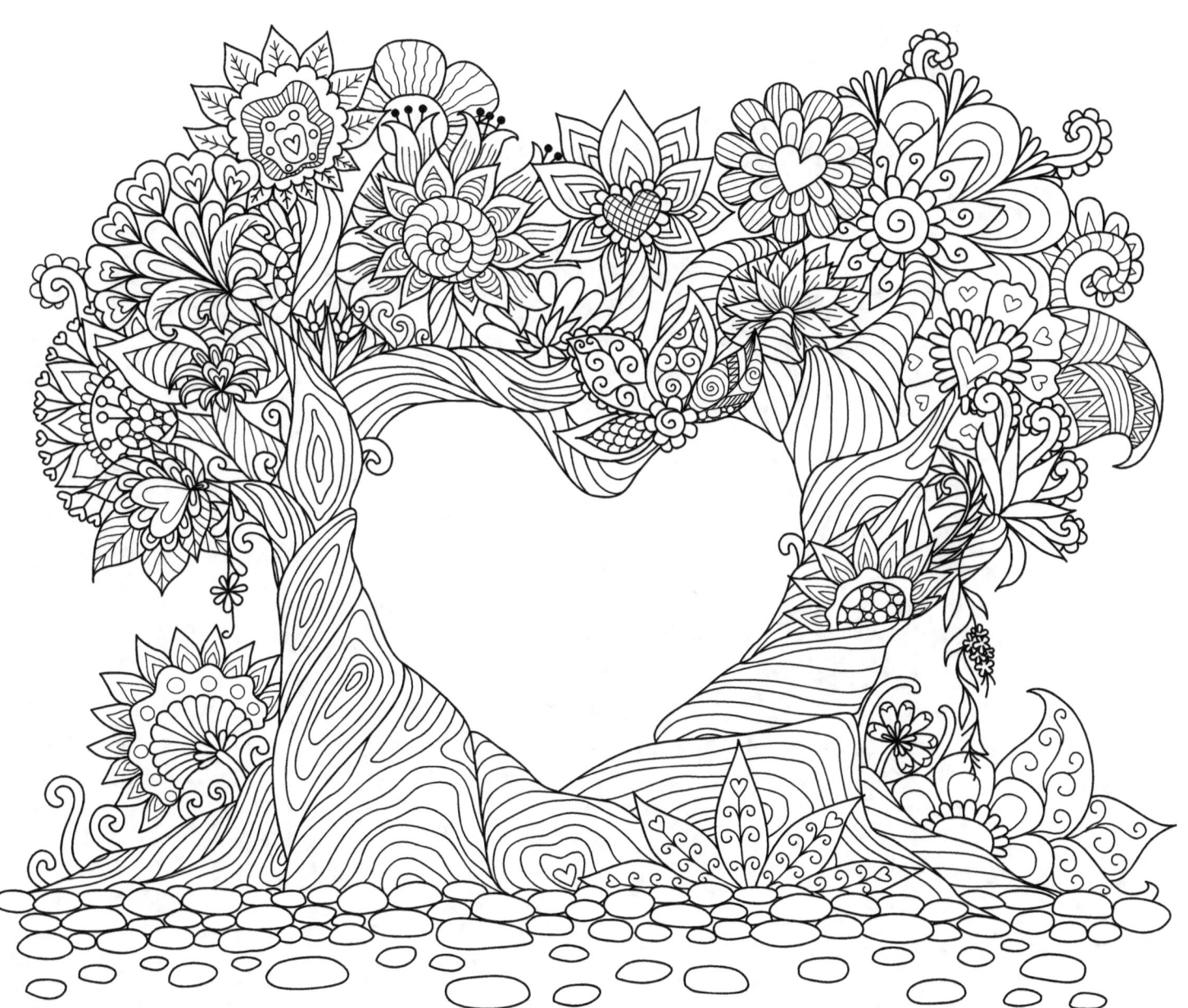

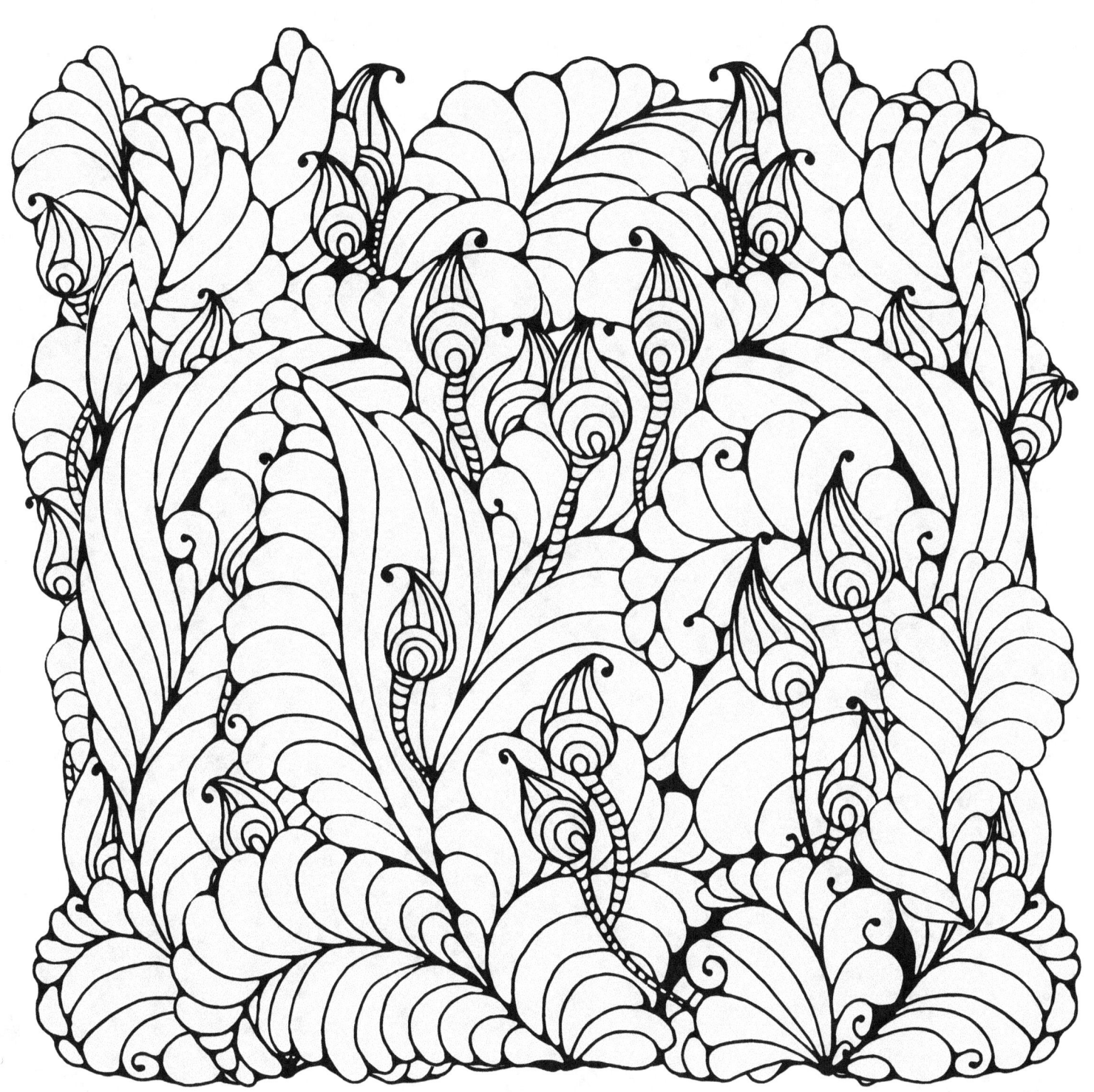

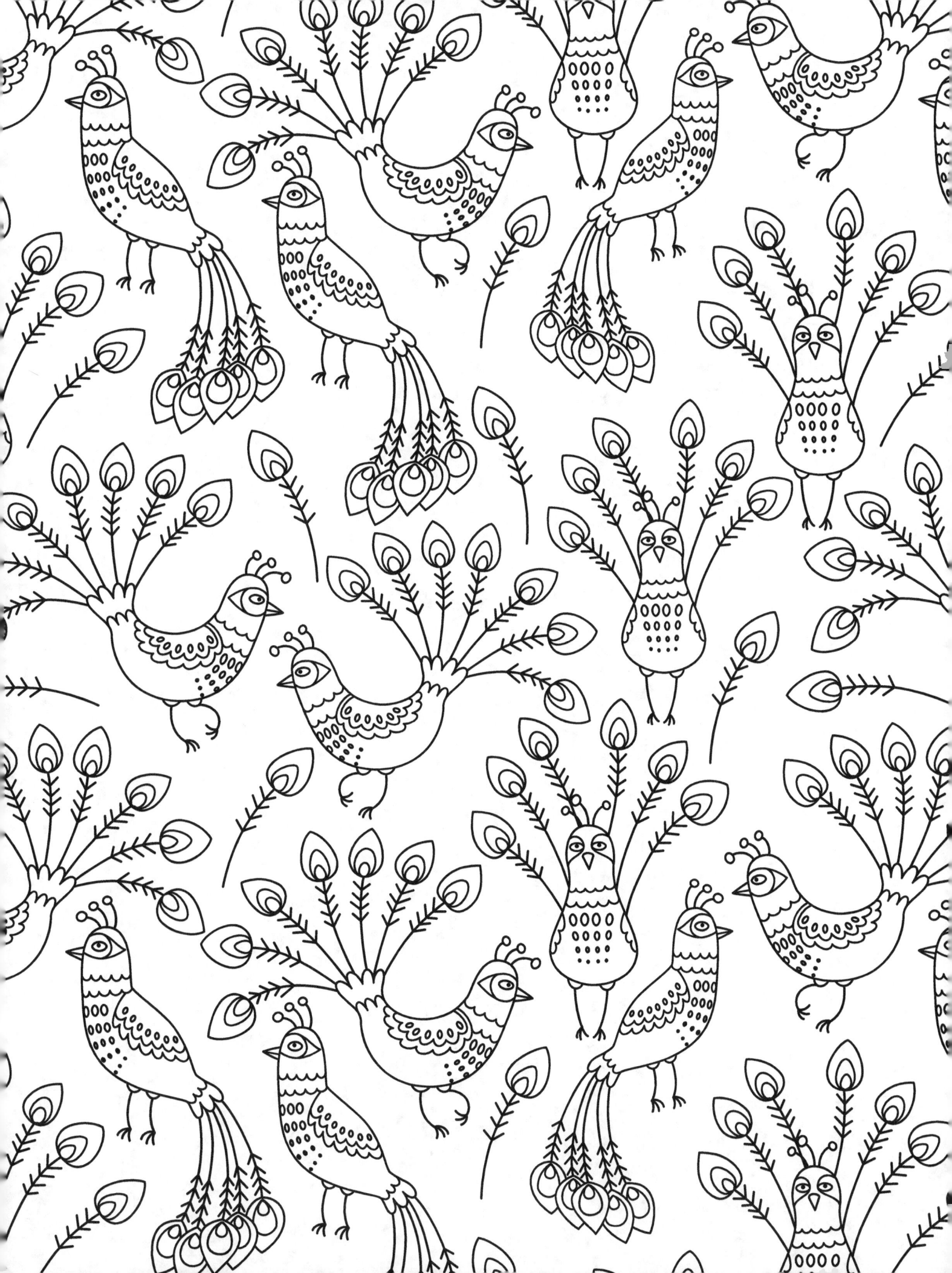

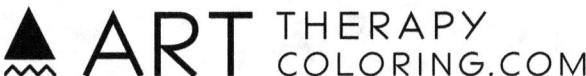

Drawings

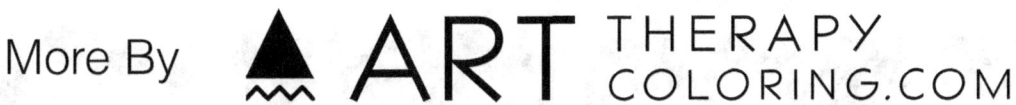
Best Selling Art Therapy Coloring Books

Coloring Books For Adults:

- Zombie Coloring Book: Black Background
- Butterfly Coloring Book For Adults: Black Background
- Tattoo Coloring Book: Black Background
- Coloring Books for Adults Relaxation: Native American Inspired Designs
- Fishing Coloring Book for Adults: Black Background

Coloring Books For Men:

- Coloring Book for Men: Anti-Stress Designs Vol 1
- Coloring Book For Men: Fishing Designs
- Coloring Book For Men: Tattoo Designs
- Coloring Books for Men: Hunting
- Coloring Book For Men: Biker Designs

Coloring Books For Seniors:

- Coloring Book For Seniors: Nature Designs Vol 1
- Coloring Book For Seniors: Anti-Stress Designs Vol 1
- Coloring Books for Seniors: Relaxing Designs
- Coloring Book For Seniors: Floral Designs Vol 1
- Coloring Book For Seniors: Ocean Designs Vol 1

Coloring Books For Teens and Tweens:

- Coloring Books For Teens: Ocean Designs
- Coloring Books for Teen Girls Vol 1
- Teen Inspirational Coloring Books
- Coloring Book for Teens: Anti-Stress Designs Vol 1
- Tween Coloring Books For Girls: Cute Animals

Coloring Books For Kids:

- Horse Coloring Book For Girls
- Coloring Books For Boys: Sharks
- Coloring Books for Boys: Animal Designs
- Unicorn Coloring Book for Girls
- Detailed Coloring Books For Kids

Art Therapy Coloring Books

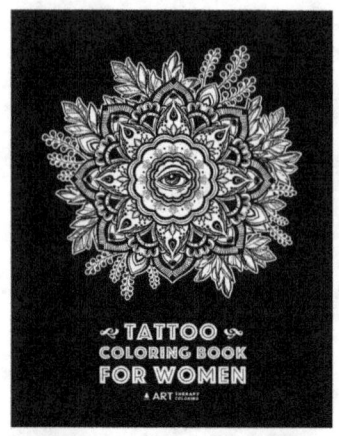

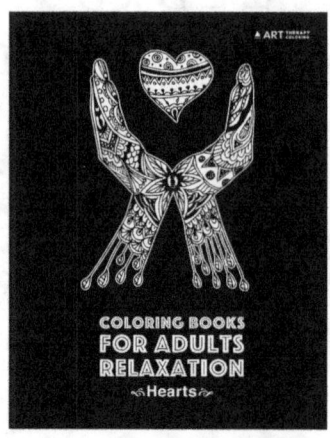

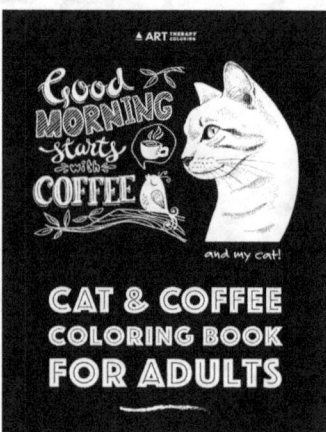

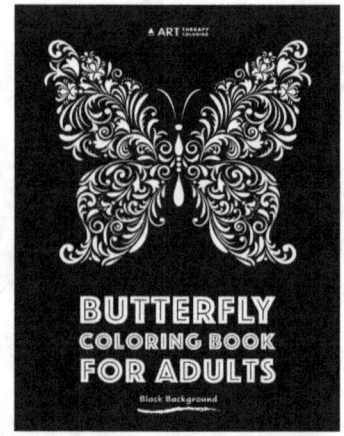

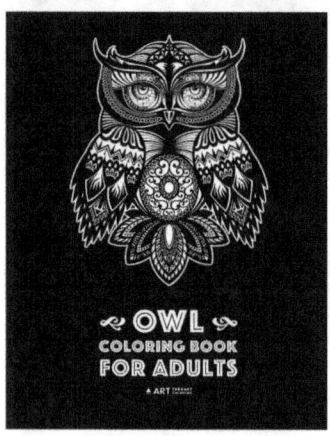

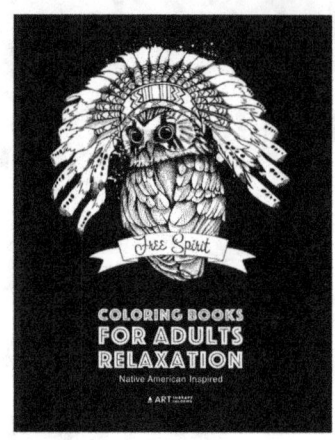

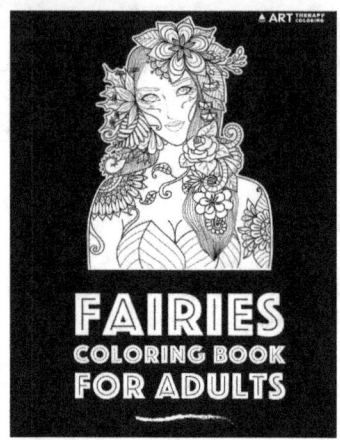

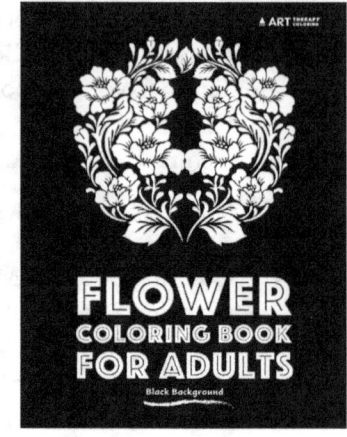

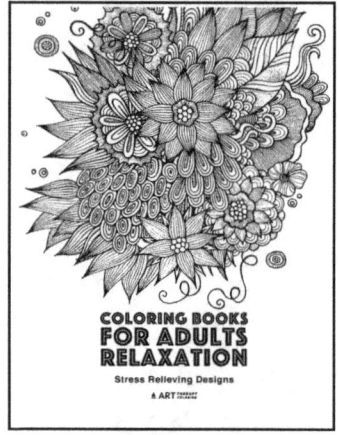

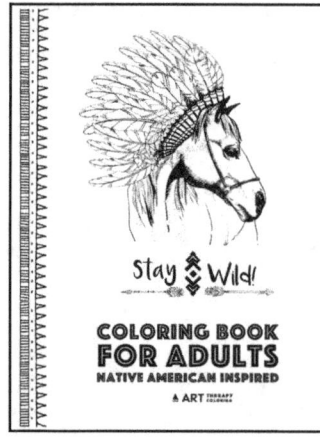

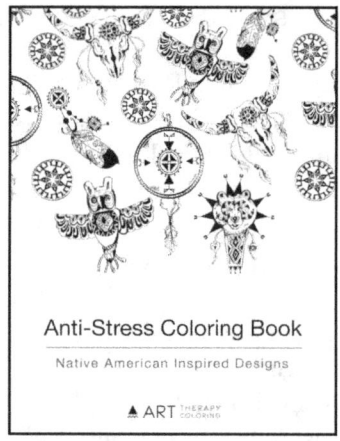

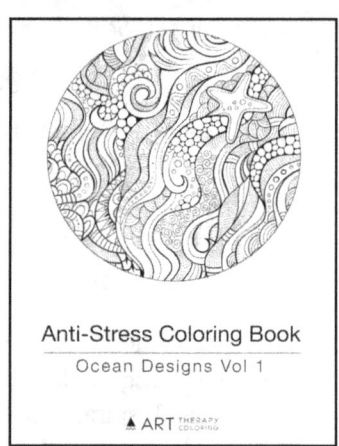

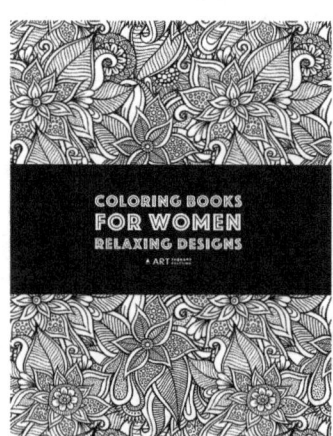

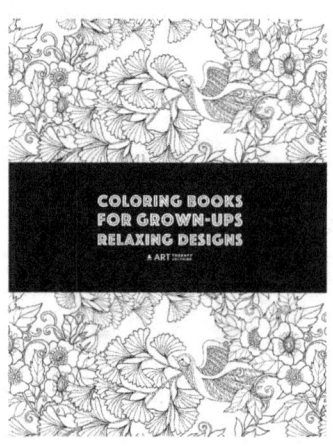

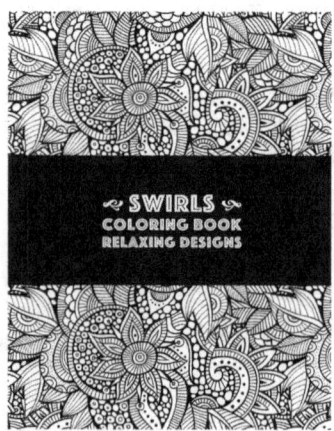

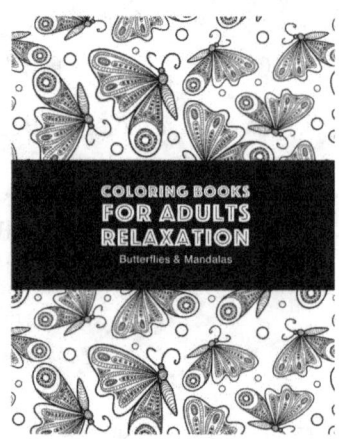

Art Therapy Coloring Books

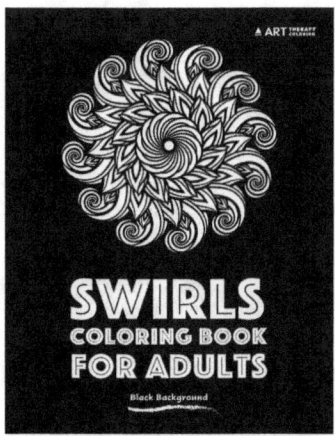

SWIRLS
COLORING BOOK
FOR ADULTS
Black Background

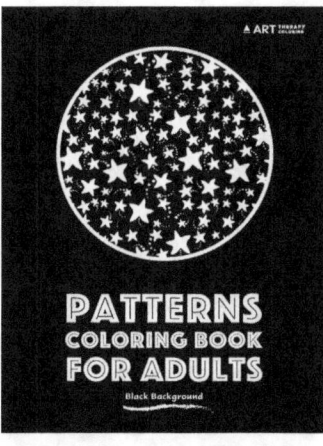

PATTERNS
COLORING BOOK
FOR ADULTS
Black Background

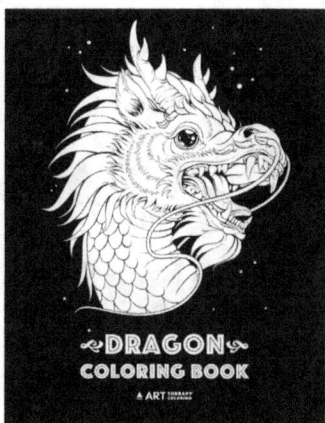

DRAGON
COLORING BOOK

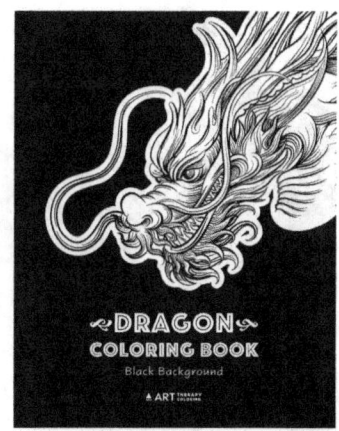

DRAGON
COLORING BOOK
Black Background

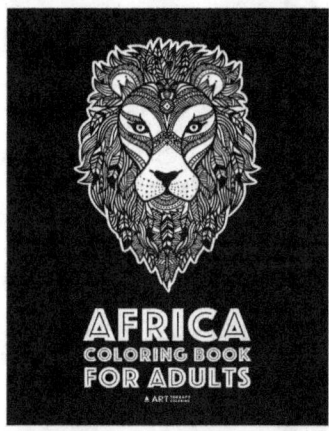

AFRICA
COLORING BOOK
FOR ADULTS

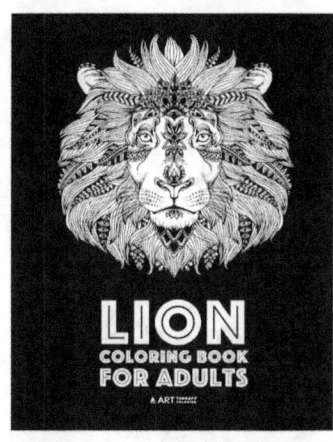

LION
COLORING BOOK
FOR ADULTS

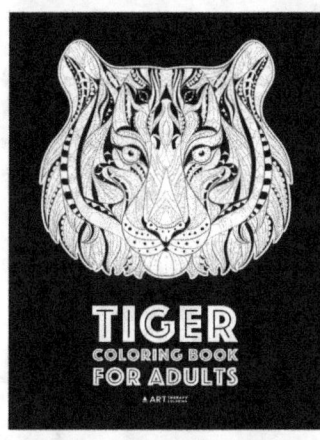

TIGER
COLORING BOOK
FOR ADULTS

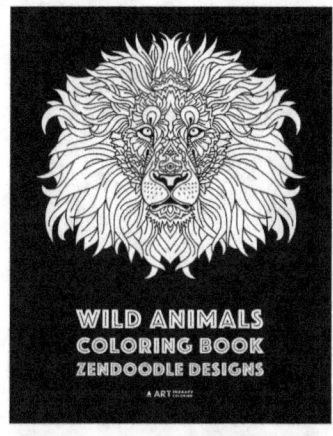

WILD ANIMALS
COLORING BOOK
ZENDOODLE DESIGNS

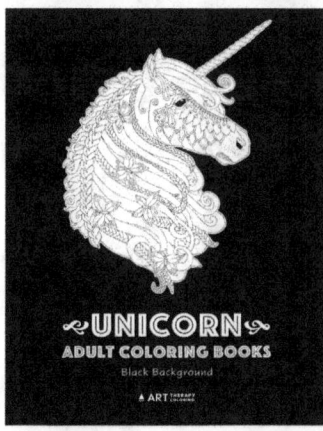

UNICORN
ADULT COLORING BOOKS
Black Background

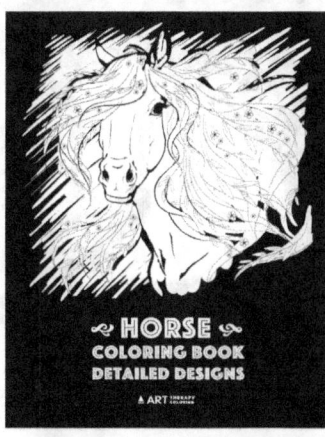

HORSE
COLORING BOOK
DETAILED DESIGNS

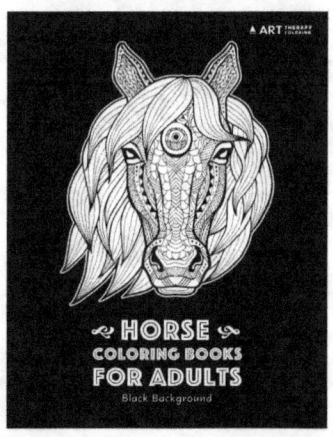

HORSE
COLORING BOOKS
FOR ADULTS
Black Background

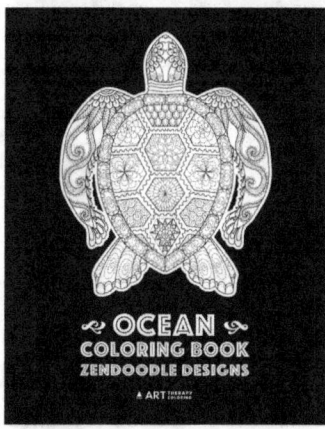

OCEAN
COLORING BOOK
ZENDOODLE DESIGNS

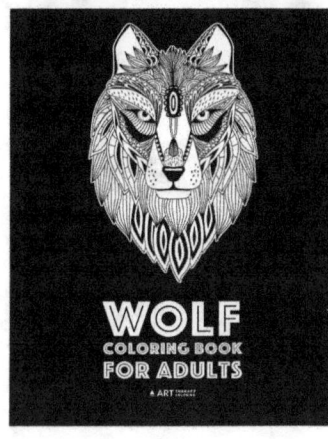

WOLF
COLORING BOOK
FOR ADULTS

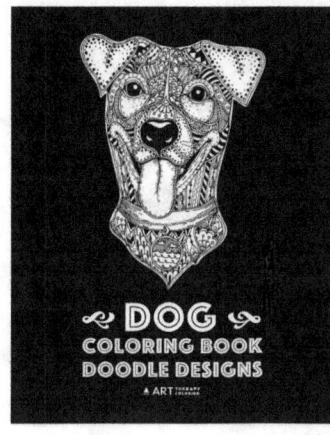

DOG
COLORING BOOK
DOODLE DESIGNS

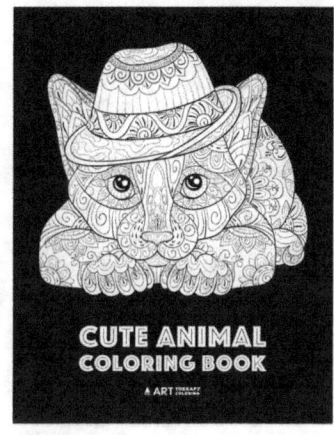

CUTE ANIMAL
COLORING BOOK

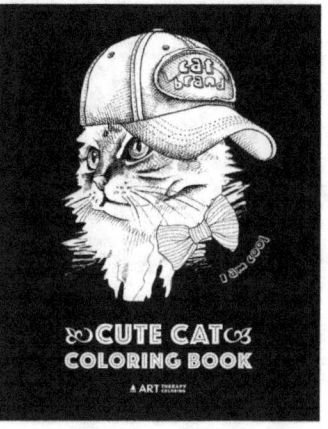

CUTE CAT
COLORING BOOK

Art Therapy Coloring Books

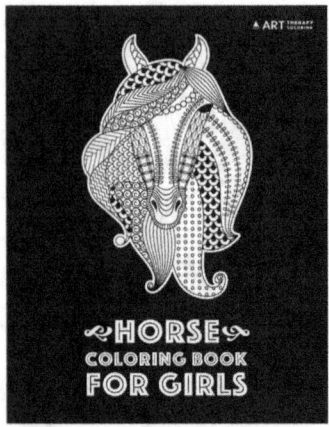

HORSE
COLORING BOOK
FOR GIRLS

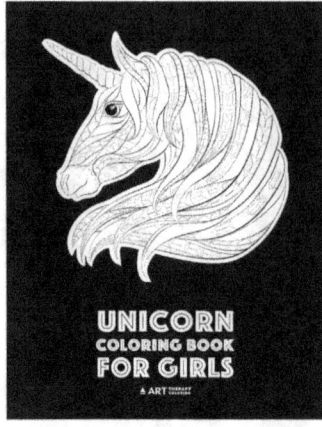

UNICORN
COLORING BOOK
FOR GIRLS

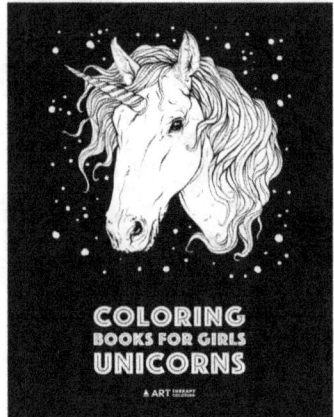

COLORING
BOOKS FOR GIRLS
UNICORNS

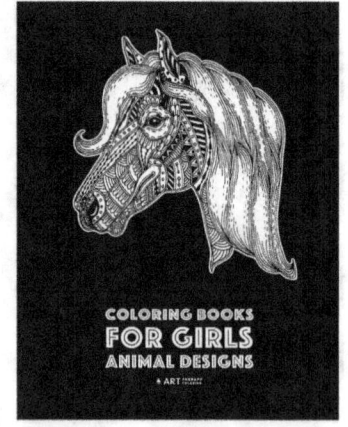

COLORING BOOKS
FOR GIRLS
ANIMAL DESIGNS

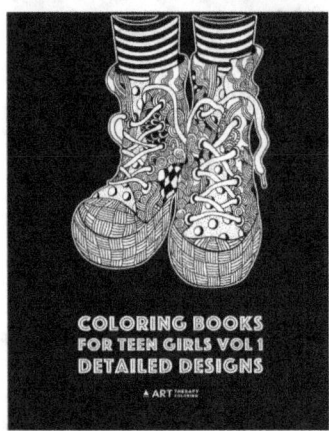

COLORING BOOKS
FOR TEEN GIRLS VOL 1
DETAILED DESIGNS

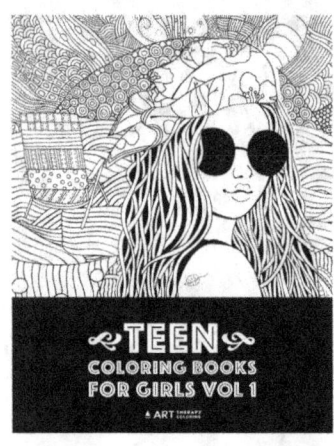

TEEN
COLORING BOOKS
FOR GIRLS VOL 1

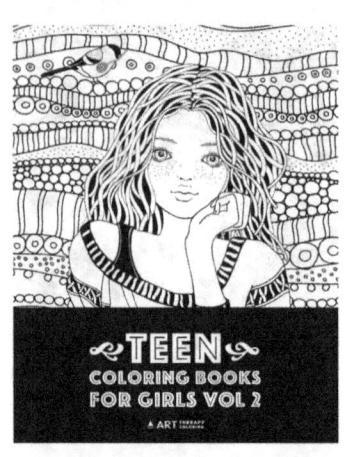

TEEN
COLORING BOOKS
FOR GIRLS VOL 2

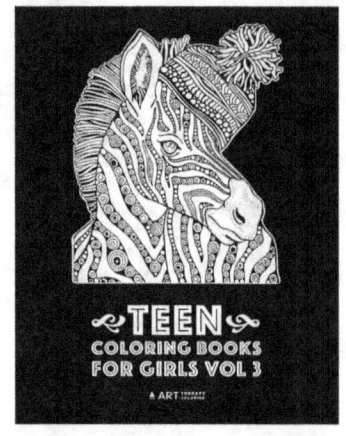

TEEN
COLORING BOOKS
FOR GIRLS VOL 3

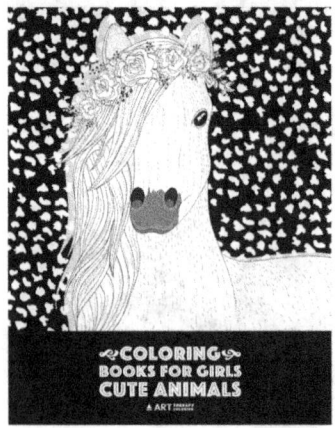

COLORING
BOOKS FOR GIRLS
CUTE ANIMALS

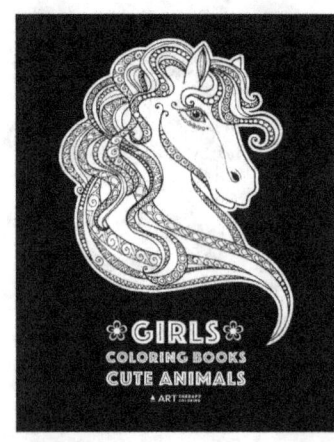

GIRLS
COLORING BOOKS
CUTE ANIMALS

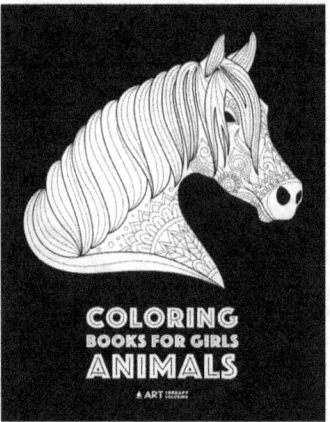

COLORING
BOOKS FOR GIRLS
ANIMALS

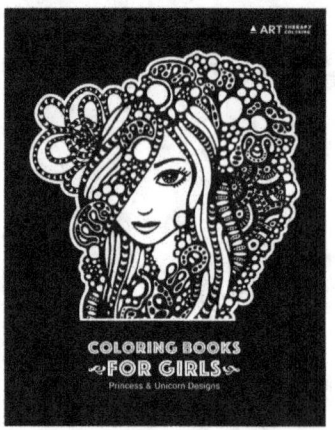

COLORING BOOKS
FOR GIRLS
Princess & Unicorn Designs

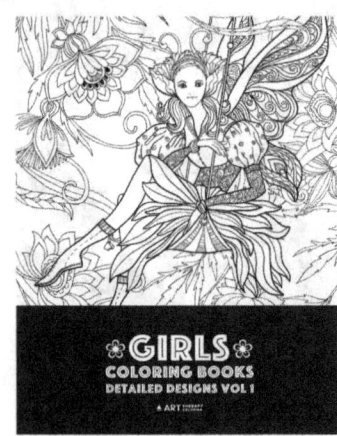

GIRLS
COLORING BOOKS
DETAILED DESIGNS VOL 1

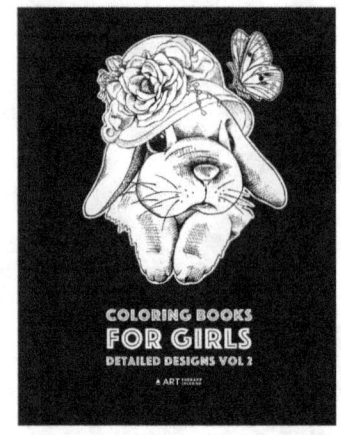

COLORING BOOKS
FOR GIRLS
DETAILED DESIGNS VOL 2

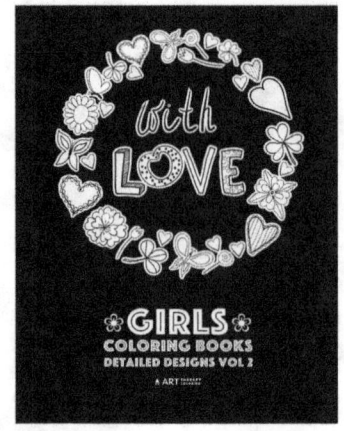

GIRLS
COLORING BOOKS
DETAILED DESIGNS VOL 2

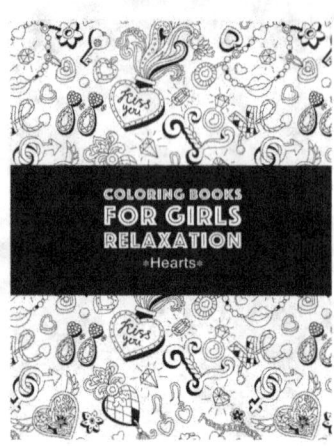

COLORING BOOKS
FOR GIRLS
RELAXATION
Hearts

Art Therapy Coloring Books

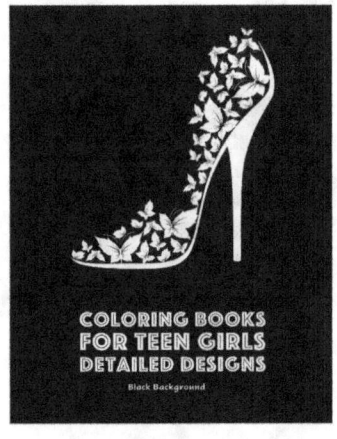

COLORING BOOKS FOR TEEN GIRLS DETAILED DESIGNS

Black Background

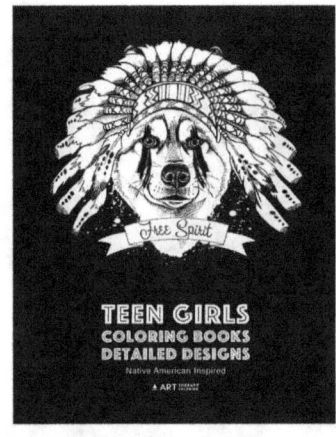

TEEN GIRLS COLORING BOOKS DETAILED DESIGNS

Native American Inspired

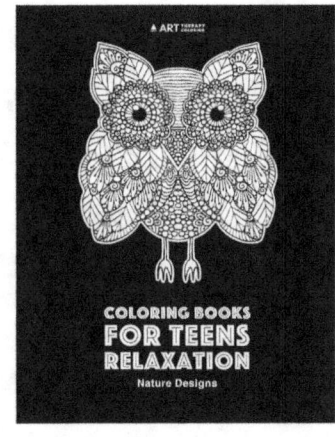

COLORING BOOKS FOR TEENS RELAXATION

Nature Designs

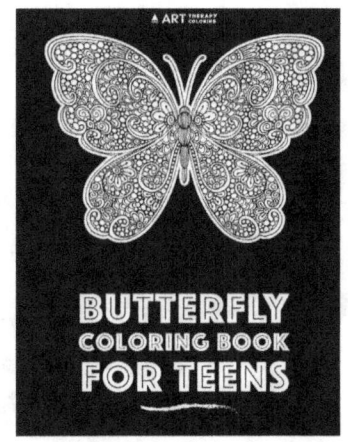

BUTTERFLY COLORING BOOK FOR TEENS

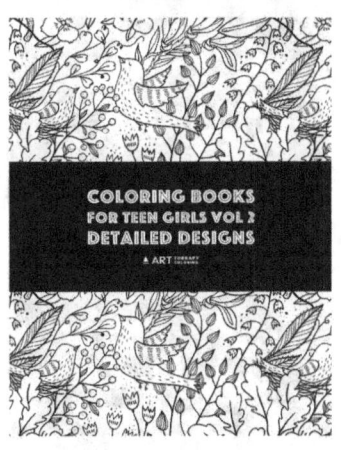

COLORING BOOKS FOR TEEN GIRLS VOL 2 DETAILED DESIGNS

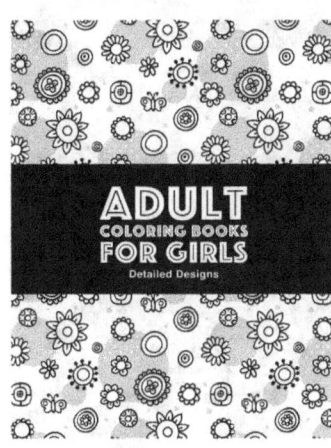

ADULT COLORING BOOKS FOR GIRLS

Detailed Designs

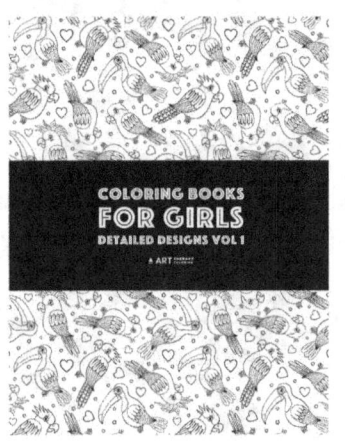

COLORING BOOKS FOR GIRLS DETAILED DESIGNS VOL I

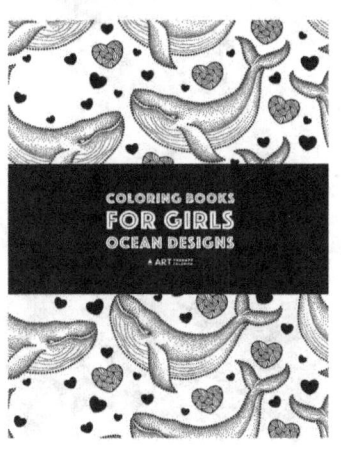

COLORING BOOKS FOR GIRLS OCEAN DESIGNS

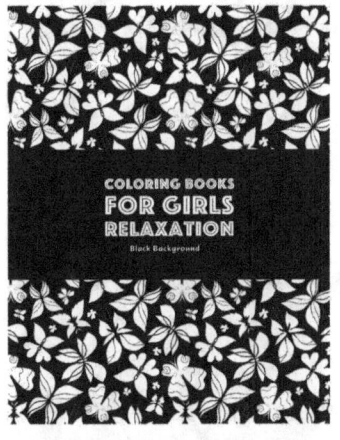

COLORING BOOKS FOR GIRLS RELAXATION

Black Background

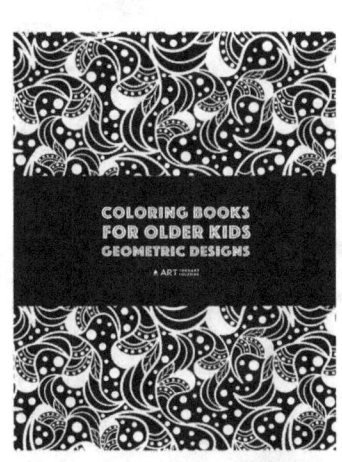

COLORING BOOKS FOR OLDER KIDS GEOMETRIC DESIGNS

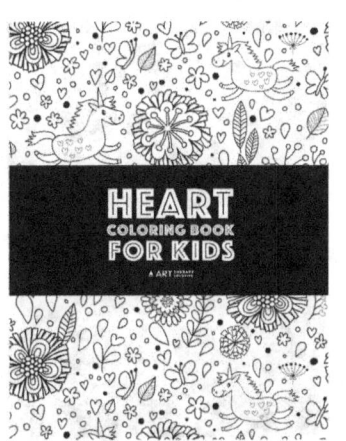

HEART COLORING BOOK FOR KIDS

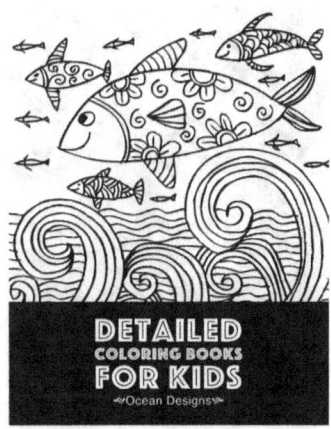

DETAILED COLORING BOOKS FOR KIDS

Ocean Designs

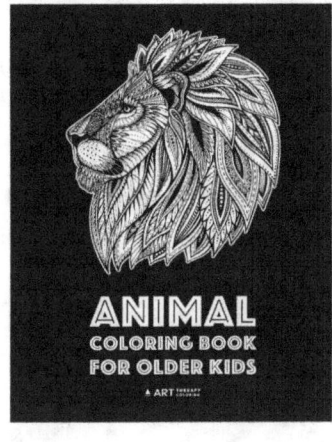

ANIMAL COLORING BOOK FOR OLDER KIDS

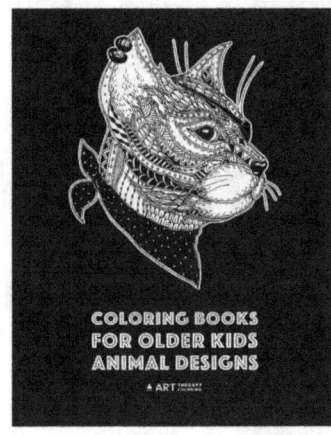

COLORING BOOKS FOR OLDER KIDS ANIMAL DESIGNS

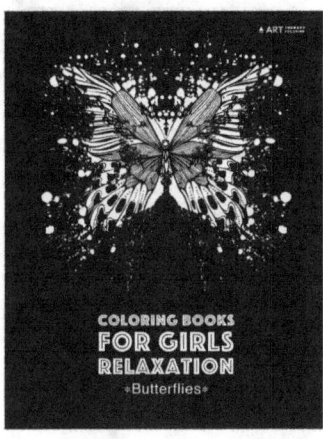

COLORING BOOKS FOR GIRLS RELAXATION

Butterflies

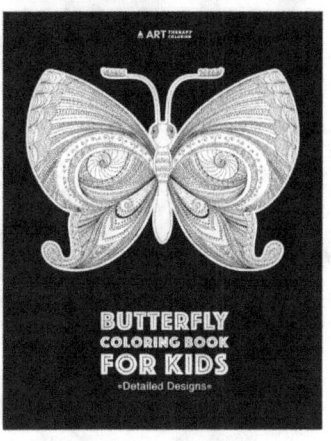

BUTTERFLY COLORING BOOK FOR KIDS

Detailed Designs

Art Therapy Coloring Books

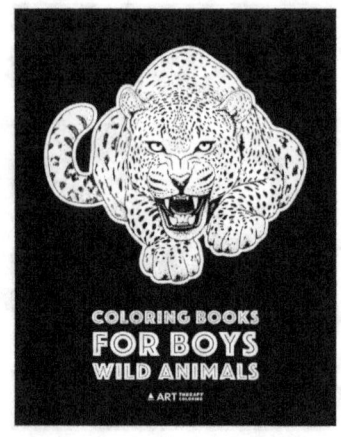

COLORING BOOKS
FOR BOYS
WILD ANIMALS

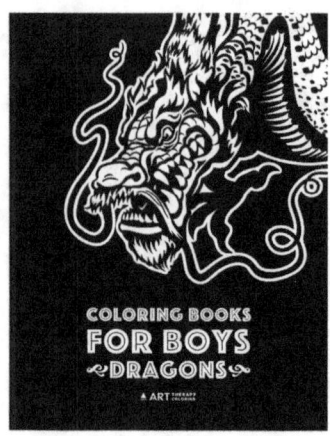

COLORING BOOKS
FOR BOYS
DRAGONS

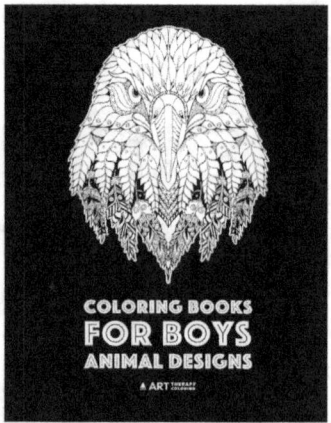

COLORING BOOKS
FOR BOYS
ANIMAL DESIGNS

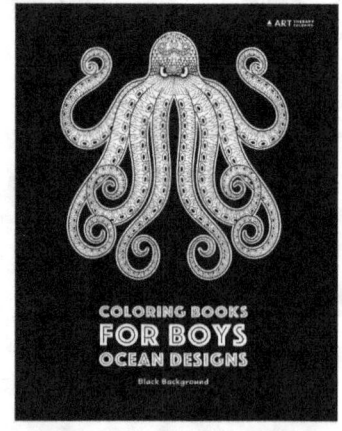

COLORING BOOKS
FOR BOYS
OCEAN DESIGNS
Black Background

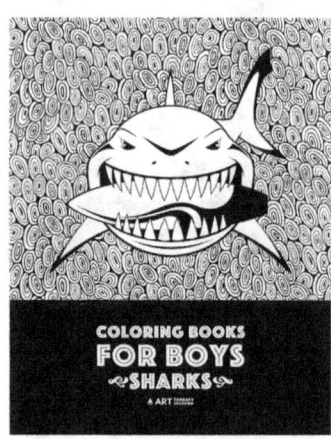

COLORING BOOKS
FOR BOYS
SHARKS

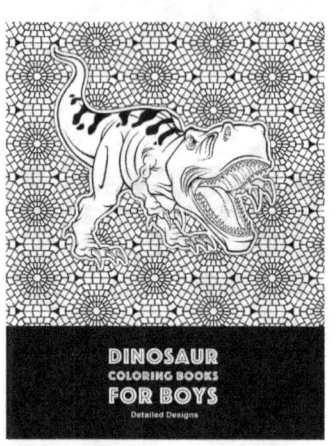

DINOSAUR
COLORING BOOKS
FOR BOYS
Detailed Designs

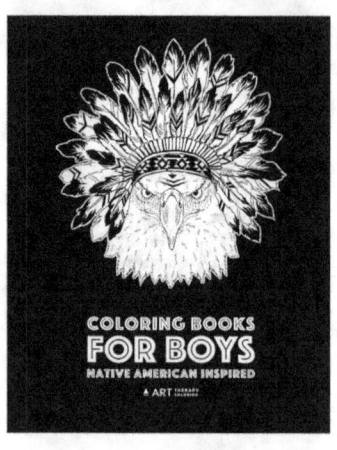

COLORING BOOKS
FOR BOYS
NATIVE AMERICAN INSPIRED

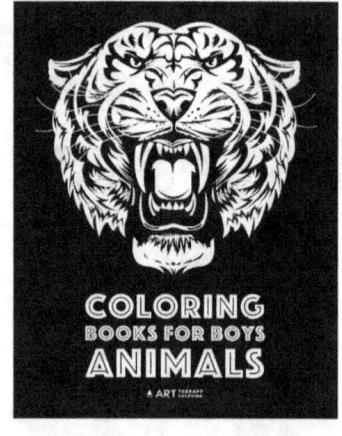

COLORING
BOOKS FOR BOYS
ANIMALS

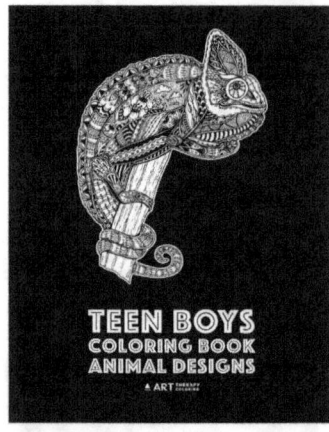

TEEN BOYS
COLORING BOOK
ANIMAL DESIGNS

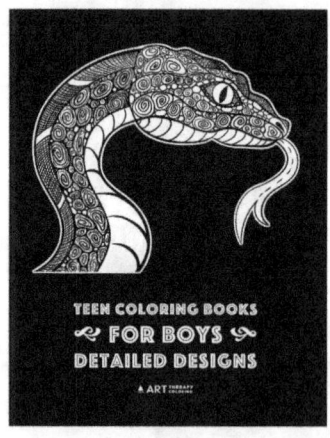

TEEN COLORING BOOKS
FOR BOYS
DETAILED DESIGNS

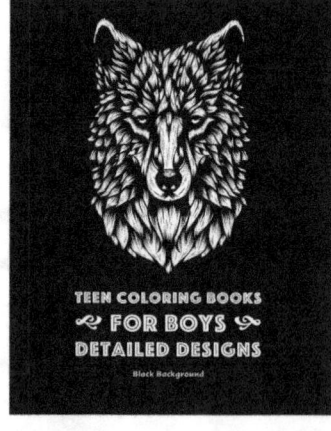

TEEN COLORING BOOKS
FOR BOYS
DETAILED DESIGNS
Black Background

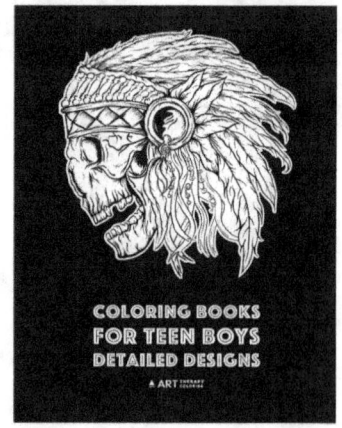

COLORING BOOKS
FOR TEEN BOYS
DETAILED DESIGNS

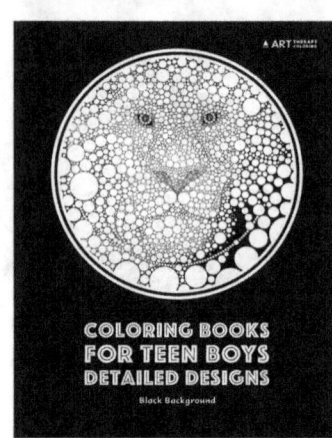

COLORING BOOKS
FOR TEEN BOYS
DETAILED DESIGNS
Black Background

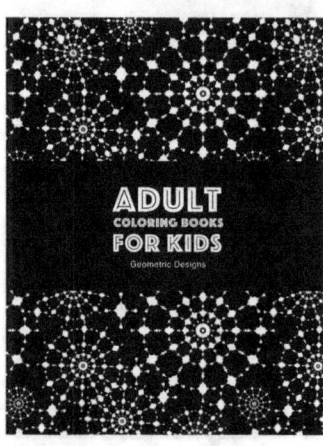

ADULT
COLORING BOOKS
FOR KIDS
Geometric Designs

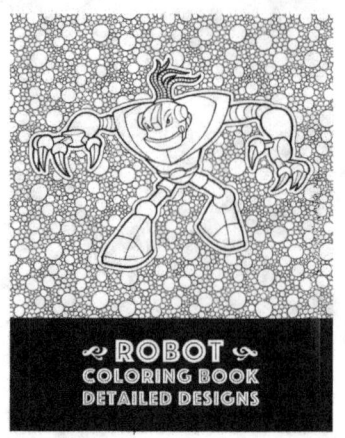

ROBOT
COLORING BOOK
DETAILED DESIGNS

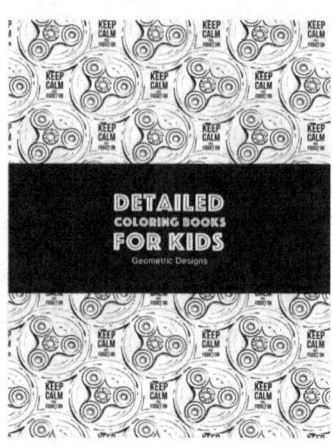

DETAILED
COLORING BOOKS
FOR KIDS
Geometric Designs

Art Therapy Coloring Books

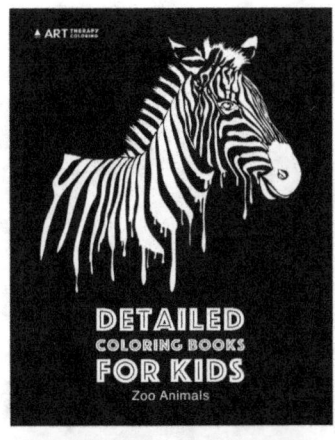

DETAILED
COLORING BOOKS
FOR KIDS
Zoo Animals

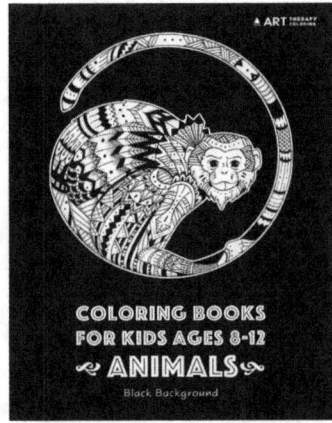

COLORING BOOKS
FOR KIDS AGES 8-12
ANIMALS
Black Background

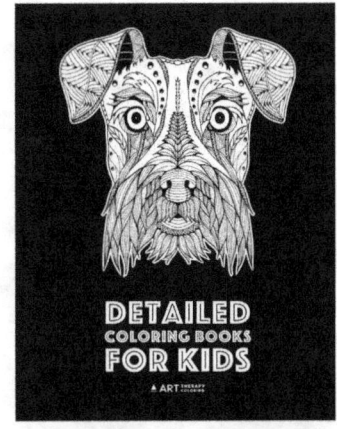

DETAILED
COLORING BOOKS
FOR KIDS

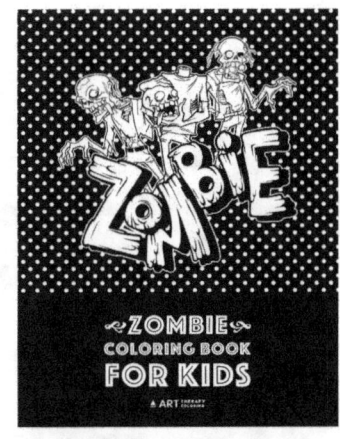

ZOMBIE
COLORING BOOK
FOR KIDS

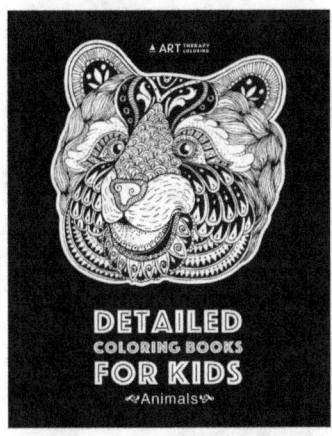

DETAILED
COLORING BOOKS
FOR KIDS
Animals

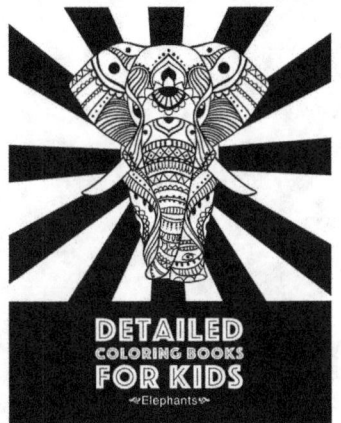

DETAILED
COLORING BOOKS
FOR KIDS
Elephants

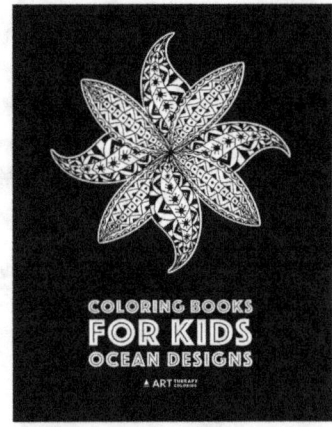

COLORING BOOKS
FOR KIDS
OCEAN DESIGNS

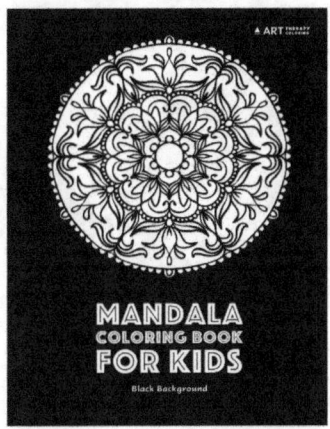

MANDALA
COLORING BOOK
FOR KIDS
Black Background

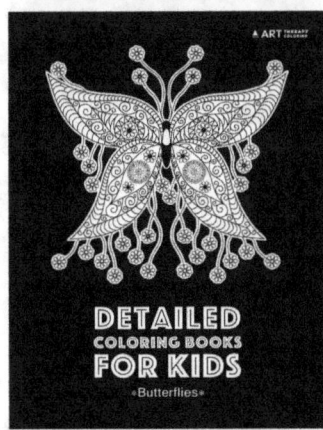

DETAILED
COLORING BOOKS
FOR KIDS
Butterflies

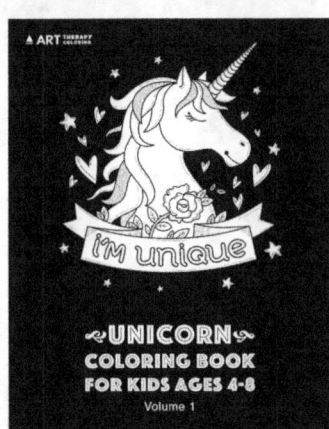

UNICORN
COLORING BOOK
FOR KIDS AGES 4-8
Volume 1

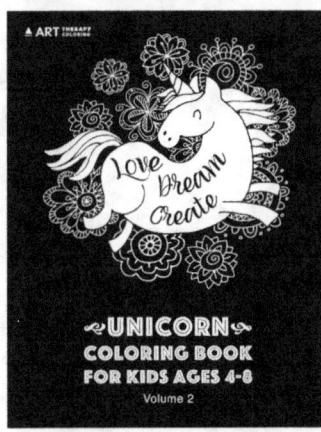

UNICORN
COLORING BOOK
FOR KIDS AGES 4-8
Volume 2

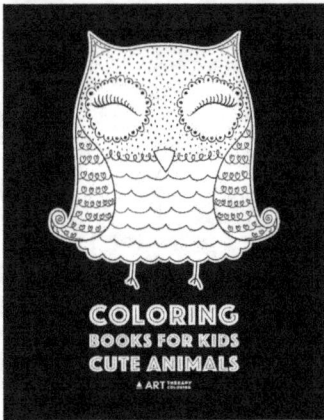

COLORING
BOOKS FOR KIDS
CUTE ANIMALS

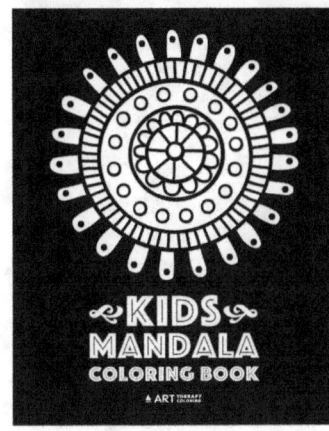

KIDS
MANDALA
COLORING BOOK

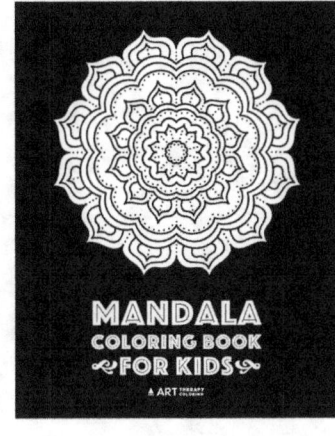

MANDALA
COLORING BOOK
FOR KIDS

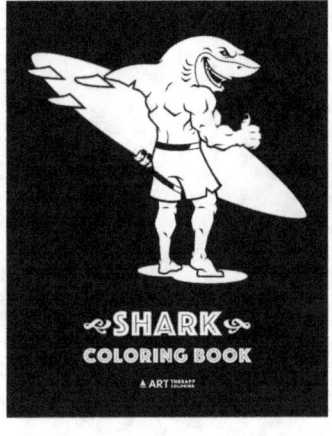

SHARK
COLORING BOOK

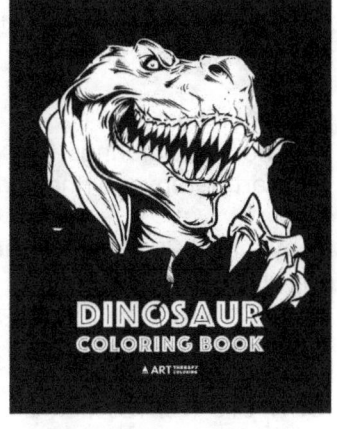

DINOSAUR
COLORING BOOK

Coloring Books For Relaxation
Anti-Stress Designs

Published by:
Art Therapy Coloring
www.arttherapycoloring.com

Shutterstock Images

ISBN: 978-1-64126-064-0